Published by
Shelby Britt

I0157106

Lies From His Heart

This is a work of fiction. Names, characters, places
and incidents either arc the product of the author's
imagination or are used fictitiously, and
resemblance to actual persons, living or dead,
business establishments, events, or locales is
entirely coincidental.

Pushing myself out of the bed with my newfound strength, I got up and prepared myself for the rest of my life. Ever since I was little, I waited to get married and find the man of my dreams. Problem was, I thought I had finally found my Prince Charming, but what I really found was a box of happily never after.

Lies from His Heart

A Novella by Picola S. Britt

Dedicated to my son, Aaron Alexander

*Aaron, without you, I would be nothing. You are the reason I wake up each morning and bust my butt so that you can have the world. One day, we will rule the world! I love you dearly, son. *You and I**

Chapter One

I slowly opened my eyes. The dried up tears that formed the night before made it difficult to focus. I tossed and turned all night because my husband of four years didn't come home after being gone all day.

The sunlight peeped its way through the blinds as I buried my head deeper into my pillow.

"I wished I was still sleep so I wouldn't have to deal with this drama," I muttered. "It's like a third person in our relationship."

I closed my eyes and inhaled the staleness of the morning air.

"This is not happening to me." I took a deep breath, letting the air seep through my nose as if I was smoking a cigarette. "What's my next move?"

I looked over at my nightstand and reached for my cell phone.

No new messages. Not even a voice mail.

I felt numb all over.

Scrolling through the recent call list, I stopped on my husband Jason's number and selected it.

"Damn!" I wiped through the corners of my eyelids and sat on the edge of the bed.

Jason's voice-mail message played, and I was almost lost in his smooth, soft deep tone. It always made my body tingle when I heard it. I couldn't believe that same voice now made my skin crawl with anger.

I sat there in silence waiting for the beep. I tried to speak, my mouth opened and closed, but no sound came out. I was beyond pissed and confused.

The phone slipped from my hand and fell on the floor, bouncing on the carpet.

"I'm supposed to be his wife, someone he loves," I said, but I felt like a fool instead of a wife.

As I moved to get up, I noticed the crumpled piece of paper I had thrown on the floor the night before. In big black bold letters, LATE NOTICE seeped through the edges of the paper and stared me in the eyes.

I had received the same type of letter three years prior and couldn't wrap my mind around why it was back in my hands again.

Instead of getting up and going to church, I sat at home on the side of my bed waiting to see what my husband's next move was. Jason knew I went to church every Sunday, so the chances of him coming back home while I was out of the house would make it easy for him to avoid any confrontation with me.

"Damn him." I pushed myself away from the bed. My mind raced as I remembered the argument that caused us to be in this sad place. I shook my head, but the memories refused to shake loose.

I walked into the bathroom and stood in front of the mirror. My brown wavy hair that fell just past my shoulders was messy and tangled. My fingers got caught each time I tried to run my hands through it, and my neck snapped back with every move. The more I moved through each strand, the more agitated I became.

"Shit!" I frowned, grabbing a rubber band and pulling the messy hair into a ponytail.

After splashing some cold water on my face, I took a step back and looked over my body in the mirror. Turning to the side and looking at my view from behind, my green eyes followed the reflection as if I was a model on a casting call. I looked good, and that wasn't me being conceited. At 33, my caramel complexion was smooth and tight and my five-foot-five frame was curved like Tyra Banks.

Moving closer to the mirror, I wiped my eyes. A tear rolled down my right cheek and dropped on the sink. I shook my head; I didn't like what I was seeing. Or what I was feeling. I was exhausted and lost. I wasn't the happy go lucky woman who said "I do" four years ago. Someone else was standing in front of the mirror, and it wasn't me. I didn't see a confident woman who knew what she wanted. I didn't see the woman who kicked asses and then took names. Before this, I was on top of the world. I had a great job as an executive for a top bridal salon and was always happy living the life of a single businesswoman. Now all I saw was someone who had been hurt, someone's whose ego was damaged, someone who tried to hold on to a marriage that should have ended a long time ago. My mind wouldn't allow me to think of anything else except for Jason.

I sat on the side of the tub, took a deep breath, and played what happened over and over in my head.

I had been standing at the mailbox, mail in hand when I lost it. In a flash, I had Jason on the phone.

I was surprised he had even answered. In addition to his job as an elementary school teacher, Jason worked as a janitor for a call center. There were only a few times in the day that I could call him, so I knew I had to call when he was on a break or getting ready to get off.

Oftentimes, when I did call him, he would say, "Baby, I'm just sitting here waiting for my shift to start." Or "What's up, baby? I'm on my lunch break."

The minute he said, "Hey baby," I was ready to leap through the phone on him.

"I just can't do this anymore," I had yelled.

"Can't do what?" he asked.

"Why am I holding a letter from the rental office?"

I heard papers shuffling around and chairs being moved. I knew he was trying to avoid the subject at hand by making a bunch of noise.

"I need you to tell me what is going on, Jason!" My voice quivered, and my tone was high.

"My boss is calling me. I gotta go," he said as he rushed me off the phone. I knew he was using that excuse so I couldn't question him, but I kept on, and I wouldn't let him hang up.

"Why do we have a late notice again, Jason?"

"I…I can't talk right now, Andrea," he said. His tone had no inflection in it. It was almost like he didn't care.

My irritation grew, and my heart rate increased. Just then, my temples started to catch on to the rhythm of my heart, and they both started to dance.

I remembered I was still standing in the front yard next to the mailbox and probably giving my neighbors great views of my drama, so I walked back up to the driveway and into the house. I rubbed my temples and closed my eyes as I pressed my cell phone tightly against my ear.

The truth was Jason didn't pay the rent and we were about to be evicted if it wasn't paid, but he wouldn't admit to it. I knew he wasn't going to give me the answers over the phone either.

I tried to keep my voice low so that my voice wouldn't carry. The warm June breeze was floating through the windows as the curtains turned inside out. I stood in the middle of the living room and rubbed my pulsating temples.

Before I knew it, I yelled, "This is my fucking life!"

Normally, I didn't curse, but Jason's ability to hide the truth from me had proven he had no respect for me.

"Are you cursing at me, Andrea?" he asked slowly as if nothing was wrong. He had no emotion in his voice, but I could tell he was hiding his feelings from me. "Look, I got to get back to work, my boss is calling me."

"You must think I'm a fool, don't you?" I lifted my hand and smacked it against my forehead. "You may as well call me stupid and write sausage head on my forehead."

The line went dead.

"Hello? Jason?" I yelled, looking at the phone.

He had hung up without me getting my answer.

I walked toward the window and stared out to the mailbox.

"God damn!" I shook my head and started to cry. I walked over to the sofa feeling disappointed and lost. Every time he hid something from me, I had to wait for him to talk to me. I felt like a child

14

having to wait for my grown ass husband to give me an answer to a question that I already knew the answer to.

And still, I waited, waited a whole day later for Jason to call me back or come home so that we could talk.

Because Jason worked some overnight shifts, he stopped going to church with me on Sundays. He would always say he was too tired or needed to rest and couldn't attend. To me, he didn't go to church because he was ashamed of what he was hiding from me. I believed, but couldn't prove that Jason didn't have the money he used to have before we got married. Maybe he was hiding the fact that he was helping his mother and giving her money. I didn't know what to believe, but who would go to church when they were not right within themselves? But the Lord did say come as you are.

But Jason didn't. I had a feeling he would come home while I was at church and quietly take all his things and leave. He had done this before, and I was going to make sure he didn't do it again.

As I sat on the living room sofa, I looked down at my pajamas. They didn't match. When I went to bed, I was so distraught and exhausted I put on anything. I had on Mickey Mouse printed valor pants that came just above my ankles and a white short sleeve 2012 tour Erykah Badu T-shirt that stopped just above my navel. Our dog Coco, a Bichon Frise who had been with us for three years, sat next to me on the sofa. She licked my hand as if it was a dog treat. I rubbed her soft white fur, and she turned over on her back so that I could rub her belly. Having her sit next to me made me feel like everything was going to be ok. I guess that's why they call dogs man's best friend.

16

I looked at her and thought, *You are my only friend*, and that thought broke me.

The kitchen doorknob clicked, and I sat straight on the sofa as if I was preparing for an interview. Coco, still licking my hand, jumped up at attention too. She knew the sound of a key rattling meant someone was coming through the door and that excited her. She jumped up and ran out of the living room into the kitchen. I sat there waiting for Jason to come into the living room, and I prepared myself for the worse.

My emotions were all over the place as my anger started to seep out my pores. I started to sweat and a little was running down the side of my neck. I knew I had to stay calm if I wanted answers from him. I put my hands on my knees and lowered my head. I inhaled, and my breath took forever to leave my body. I wanted to have a sense of calm, but I couldn't find it. I looked around the room to find something that would give me peace, but all I could focus on was the Bible that sat near the front door. I sat it there Saturday nights before I went to bed so I wouldn't forget it the next morning for church.

I wanted to cry. My hands felt wet and were shaking. I was a nervous wreck. Five minutes had passed, and Jason had not come into the room. This upset me, so I jumped up and stormed into the kitchen with a look of disgust on my face.

Jason sat at the kitchen table, his head down as he held Coco. He still had his work clothes on and his slim, fitted, navy button down shirt was half tucked, and his beige Sean Jean belt hung loose on his medium frame. His eyes were red and had bags under them. That told me that he hadn't had much sleep. He looked as though he was about to take his last breath. This made me soften until I remembered

18

the emotional weight that was placed on my heart with his lies. The anger in me had reached its boiling point and the kettle was ready to whistle.

"So you're just going to come in and act like nothing is wrong?" I asked sarcastically. I had hoped for a quick response as I stood there with my hands on my hips and my leg shaking from nervousness. But when he opened his mouth, nothing but whispers came out. My blood started to boil. He rubbed his rugged salt and pepper beard and looked away from me.

"I don't know what to say, except I'm sorry...I, I messed up," he said.

Coco jumped out of his arms and started to rub up against his legs. He picked her back up and slowly started rubbing her face. She licked his hands with adornment. As I watched their interaction, I became jealous. Far be it from me to be jealous of an animal, but the way Jason gave Coco attention made my blood boil. Here I was his wife, the woman who lay next to him (almost) every night, and I could barely get an audible word out of him.

"What in the world is going on with you?" I stood in front of him with my hands in the air like I was praying. "What happened to communication? This is just too much for me. I can't keep going through this. I can't trust you anymore!"

I walked away from him as he held his head down, still rubbing the dog. I sat on the sofa and waited for a response. It was like he had just given up on us. The only question I had was "why?" It was like he didn't care. He walked in the room, standing as tall as a tree with his six-foot-two, 150-pound frame. He towered over me like a building and that frightened me. I noticed that he now seemed alert and ready to talk. For a minute, I thought he was going to come clean about what he was doing, and then he opened his mouth.

"Maybe you need to look at how you talk to me! It's all about love. That's what's going on, Andrea."

I looked up at him and cocked my head to the side. I opened my eyes wide so he could see I was serious. I used to look at Jason and his brown eyes and melt. That was the first thing that attracted me to him when we first met five years ago, but today his eyes were dark. He loomed over me as if he was king of the castle, a title he had been failing to fill. Confused but remaining calm, I kept my voice low and stared at him.

"Don't turn this around on me. I did nothing wrong," I said. "This is all about what you did and why we are in this situation."

21

I put my hand against my chin and felt the hot steam coming from my neck. I put my hands over my eyes so he wouldn't see that my eyes were filling up with tears. Wiping them quickly, I took a breath and quietly said, "If I can't trust you, there is nothing left."

My head hung down, and I stared at the floor. The words ran out of my mouth and slapped him in the face. He stood there startled. He looked at me and shook his head.

"Well, if you can't trust me, then we don't need to be together."

Mixed in with softness was a bit of hatred. I used to love that about him. His tone was always deep and low, but soft. Even when he raised his voice, it was a calming sound for my ears. But the way he spoke to me this time was like I was hearing another person. His words pierced my heart. And it hurt. His face told me he was relieved that our relationship was almost over, but he still didn't tell me why he hadn't paid the rent. Secretly, I knew he wouldn't tell me about what he had done, and I realized I probably never would find out why. After all these years of being married, it was going to be left to one question that I would never get the answer to. I had threatened him numerous times with leaving him because of him not paying the rent on time, but was too afraid to actually go through with it. Now it was really happening. I looked at him and gulped.

"Well, there ya go," I said, throwing my hands up. "I guess we are getting a divorce." The words flew out of my mouth and stung him like a bee. With a blank look in his eyes, he rubbed his salt and pepper mustache and tried to process each word individually. He turned and walked away, disappearing to the stairs to the bedroom without looking back. I didn't follow him even though I wanted to.

I sat shaking my head because I knew what he was doing. I could hear him pacing in the bedroom. He was packing his stuff, again.

Staring down at my cell phone, I sat in silence waiting to see what was going to happen next. Ten minutes later, he walked downstairs with his gym bag on his shoulder. Some of his shirts and socks were hanging out of the side. It looked like he had stuffed as much as the bag would hold. The words "Just Do It" on the side of the bag were so stretched by what was inside the bag the letters would probably peel off soon. Around his neck was a black leather Gucci belt and a blue wool bathrobe that he wore every day. His favorite *Beats by Dre* headphones that I bought him for Christmas when we first met were tucked under his arm along with a book he had been reading about the stock market. He didn't make contact with me as he came storming down the stairs. Each step was rushed as if he had somewhere to be and fast. I looked up and put my head down, trying not to laugh because he reminded me of Steve Martin in the movie *The Jerk.* Even though I felt horrible, my ability to think about something funny made me feel a little better.

"I'll be back to get the rest of my stuff later," he said as the bass in his voice beat through my heart like a drum. I felt like a stalker as I watched his every move, back and forth through the living room and into the kitchen taking his things to the car. My mind flashed to all the memories we had together. The times I stood in the kitchen and watched him cook us meals. The days he lay on the floor playing with Coco while I sat on the sofa smiling at them both. When all the memories faded, he looked like a stranger to me.

Without hesitation, he walked back down the steps into the living room and didn't bother to look at me. He stood in front of me and looked down at the floor and then slowly turned to look at the kitchen door. And at that very moment, my marriage of only four years was over. The butterflies in my stomach were fluttering away, and my heart was beating a mile a minute. This was really happening. His chest rose up and down, and he turned and walked out on me as if he had somewhere else more important to be. Just as the door was closing behind him, I knew I had to get something off my chest. This was not over. I had to have the last word. In a moment of panic and a last resort to get him to talk to me, the words flew out of my mouth like a fighter jet.

"You are less of a man to leave me here to deal with all of this!"

And just like that, he was gone. I sat back down on the sofa and cried. My heart was broken, and the world "failure" filled my mind. I felt like less of a wife because my husband didn't love me enough to save our marriage. Tears fell out of my eyes. I didn't know if I was crying because my marriage was over, or if I was crying because now I was alone. Was I crying because now I had to explain to people that my marriage was over? Maybe I was crying because I didn't know how I was going to pay all the bills by myself. Or maybe I was crying because I was finally getting out of a relationship that I was miserable in for so long. Every scenario ran through my mind. What was I going to tell my family? How would I tell them that this man had let me down again and was now gone

27

for good? In less than five minutes, my world was already crumbling.

I took a deep breath, picked up my cell phone, and called his mother. I didn't have the best relationship with Mrs. Jerry and hardly ever saw her. Every so often, I would call her and say hi, but it was awkward and she never had much to say during our conversations. For as long as we had been married, I never stepped a foot inside Mrs. Jerry's home and didn't have a desire to. She was a smoker, and I didn't want to smell like smoke when I left her home, so I avoided the visit anytime I could. There were times when I would say to Jason that I thought she didn't like me, but he would never address it with me. He avoided the conversation, and I would eventually stop asking about her.

Nevertheless, I picked up the phone to let her know her son was on his way to her house. She answered the phone on the first ring.

"Hi, Mrs. Jerry," I said. My breathing was slow, and my tone was low.

"Hey" was all she said. Her words were short, and her tone was raspy. I cringed with every sound that came from her. I guess when you smoke all your life, your voice takes a beating. Right now she sounded like a cat hissing outside of a window.

"Your son is on his way home." The cell phone was pressed against my right ear, and I sat quietly waiting for her to say how sorry she was that this was happening to us. But she didn't. I was amazed at what she said next.

"Well," she said as I could hear the phlegm cracking in her voice, "it takes two in a relationship, and he can't do this by himself."

I wanted to come through the phone and snatch the cigarette out of her mouth! Without losing my temper, I took a breath and with no increase in my tone said, "Ok."

As much as I tried to hold them back, my emotions took the best of me, and my voice started to quiver. As she was hanging up, I managed to say, as my throat felt like it was about to close, "I did the best I could to love your son and communicate with him. I did nothing wrong!" Wiping my eyes, the lump grew bigger in my throat as I swallowed.

I waited for a response, hoping for a little bit of love and maybe some understanding, but I got nothing. She had already hung up. I stared at my phone and asked, "Why did I even call her?" I was sure she was finally happy that we were breaking up, the old bat. I looked around and felt the emptiness in the room that would soon engulf this house. My body felt cold, and I was scared and alone. Dropping to my knees, I closed my eyes and prayed. I held myself as my throat tightened. I might have lost my husband, but I still had God.

The tears flowed from my eyes as I whispered, "Lord, help me. Lord, help me." I rocked back and forth. I was weak. I stood up and fell back to my knees and wept. I wept like I had lost everything. I wept because I didn't know whom to turn to. My body was limp, and my face flushed and red. Gaining my composure, I stood back up and looked at the clock. It was noon. Slowly, I walked upstairs into our bedroom. I looked around and saw no traces of him. I sat on the bed, a bed that would now be empty. I needed to sleep. I was tired and hurt. I just wanted to sleep. I laid back and pushed my head deep into the pillow and stared at the wall. I felt Coco jump on the bed and nestle herself against my legs.

Five minutes later, I was sleeping and my husband was gone.

Chapter Two

Three years prior, I had what I thought was the perfect marriage. Jason and I hardly ever argued. After living with my parents while we saved money, we were able to find a two-bedroom apartment. Our bills were paid, and we were living a good newlywed life. We would watch TV together on the sofa and laugh together. Twice a month, we would go out to eat or have a movie date. Because he loved to cook, Jason would always cook dinner for me and take care of cleaning the kitchen, and I would take care of cleaning the rest of the house. We were content being with each other. Yes, we had ups and downs here and there, but what marriage didn't? We decided we wanted more space and privacy, so we both agreed to look for a house. After months of searching, we found the house of my dreams: a five bedroom, two-story brick home, with a big front yard. We didn't have much of a backyard, but because we didn't have small children, I knew it wouldn't bother me. Although he worked as a school teacher part time, Jason knew he needed a second job to help with the bills. He was lucky enough to find a new job working in hotel management, and wanted us to rent until we were stable financially to purchase a home. As long as we were not living with our parents, I didn't care.

"Stop the car!" I shouted.

Excitement filled the car as we passed by the house with the red door.

"That's it," I said. "I love it." My eyes widened as I gazed out the window.

Because he was a man of very little words, Jason shook his head, and in a low tone murmured what he always said, "Nice."

I closed my eyes and saw myself standing at the front door turning the key. I knew just by the look of it that this was *my* house.

"Call the number and see how much the rent is and if we can get it," I said.

He dialed the number, but he was hesitant as if he knew something I didn't about the house.

"So it's fourteen hundred dollars a month, for everything?" He glanced over at me, and I smiled. Jason talked with her for about five minutes before hanging up. He turned to me again and said, "She will call me after the credit check."

I didn't want to get too excited because I wanted to make sure this was really going to happen. Living at my parents' house would be depressing, and I needed to be in my own space.

"Do you think you can afford that amount if I pay everything else?" I asked. "I don't want us to be here struggling."

With a straight face, he looked at me and said, "We should be ok."

Sometimes I could never tell what he was thinking. He was always serious and only laughed when he thought something was really funny. Maybe the possibility of independence clouded my judgment, but my anticipation made up for his lack of approval. But, then again, he said he would be ok, so I believed him.

Weeks later, we were approved, and one month and a half later, I was in my new home with the red door. I worked hard to make our house a home. I jumped right into being the best employee at work during the week while decorating the house on the weekends. Jason concentrated on working longer hours at work to make sure the rent was being paid on time. I never questioned whether or not he paid the rent because I figured he just did. I paid all the other bills to take the strain off of him. I didn't have a problem doing this because I had a good job and I always had money left over at the end of every payday.

I loved walking into the house and seeing Jason laid back, relaxed and comfortable watching TV. Sometimes, he seemed distant, but I thought it was just the long hours at work getting to him. Nevertheless, I continued on with my daily tasks.

Just as we settled into the normalcy of being on our own again, I started to notice that Jason was coming home from work early, or either not going to work at all. Sometimes he would say he was using a vacation day.

"What are you doing here this early?" I asked as I walked into the kitchen from work. The aroma of green peppers and hamburgers filled my nostrils. Inhaling the sweet smell of melted cheese, I put down my briefcase and kicked off my two-inch black patent leather shoes. "I thought you worked till six o'clock today?"

Wiping his hands with paper towels, he smiled and moved away from the stove. In his left hand, he carried a paper plate with three cheeseburgers and three buns. Three green peppers rested on the side of the buns.

Jason sat down at the kitchen table, and I stood there waiting for an answer.

"Class ended early today because of SOL testing, so I was able to leave early." He smiled at me again, raised the burger to his mouth, and took a big bite. I didn't know what to feel. I took a breath and allowed the mixture of grease and smoke to fill my lungs.

Irritated, I let out a quick "ok" and walked out of the kitchen and into the family room. Sitting on the sofa looking at the TV, I could hear him moving around in the kitchen. I tried to figure out if there was a different reason that he was home, but I didn't feel like dealing with it, so I said nothing. I never had a real reason to question him, so I never said anything.

I made myself believe that because of the way we managed our home, happiness would fall into our laps. I was wrong.

Days turned into weeks, and Jason began to look different. His pants seemed looser than usual and his facial hair began to grow wild. He was not the man I married. We didn't go out as often as we used to, and I felt like I was doing things all by myself. Whenever we went out to dinner, I paid. I never questioned it because I was the one with the extra money.

I couldn't shake the feeling that something was wrong. Conversations around the house ceased, and Jason hid what was going on. As time went on, questions began to linger in my mind.

Was he cheating? Have I done something wrong?

I began feeling like I was alone in this marriage. I was swimming underwater, and I couldn't breathe. I didn't know what to think.

Weeks later, after a long night at work, I drove into the garage to find his car once again parked.

"Here we go again," I said, shaking my head. "Let's see what story I get tonight."

All the rooms in the house were dark. I stood at the bottom of the stairs and saw the light from the TV dancing around.

He's in the bed, I thought as I took what seemed like a long walk up the stairs to our bedroom. I became angry as I stood in the doorway and watched him lay on the bed holding the remote.

I blew a breath and asked, "Did you call the electric company to get an extension like I asked you?"

The stench of musk slapped me as I stepped into the room. I knew he had been in the same spot all night.

Stretching, and without saying a hello, he said what I always heard him say: "No, not yet."

Frowning, I mumbled, "Damn" and walked out of the room, leaving him to go back to his position of holding the remote and staring at the TV.

Reaching the bottom step, I heard him yell out to me, "I made dinner, it's in the oven."

I used to come home and we would sit and talk or watch TV together. Now he just lay around like a bump on a log. I couldn't shake the feelings I had. I was paranoid and didn't have anyone I trusted to tell my feelings to. I didn't want anyone to talk about me behind my back or tell me I was being stupid, so I kept my feelings to myself. My heart was hurting, but I didn't tell Jason. Even when he would kiss me goodbye in the morning on his way to work, I never let on that something didn't feel right. I hid my emotions just like he hid his.

Denial is a bitch!

After sitting in the kitchen most of the night thinking, I went upstairs and got in the bed. He flinched as the breeze from the comforter moved past his face when I slid in the bed. He didn't seem to notice or care that I was lying next to him.

I stared at the ceiling. My chest rose up and down as my heartbeat allowed me to drift off to sleep. As I slept, I felt a warm dry breeze run past my cheek. I opened my eyes and looked over at the nightstand next to my bed. Red lights flashed 4:30 a.m. I knew my morning kiss from Jason was soon coming. Like clockwork, after taking a shower and getting dressed, he would walk over to my side of the bed and kiss me goodbye.

"See you later," he said, kissing me softly and waiting for me to respond.

Most of the time, I would be asleep and not know he was gone. Other times, I would open one eye as he walked out of the room, not responding to him. I was just glad he was going to work. Driving an hour to his job, he would get off at six in the evening. My job, on the other hand, had me working at various hours. Sometimes, I would have to be at work at 10 a.m., but that day, I didn't have to work until two in the afternoon.

Every morning, I woke up at 9 a.m. After taking a shower, I dressed and went downstairs to the kitchen and fixed myself breakfast. With breakfast done, I walked around the house thinking about what else I could buy to add to the current décor. Standing in the living room, my eyes went from wall to wall. A cherry wood dining table stood in the middle of the floor. While gazing at the new brown leather sofa I had ordered a month before we moved in, I started to run my hands over the cushion. The soft texture of the leather was like silk.

I only had an hour before I was to leave for work, so I knew I had to get myself prepared to leave.

I heard a car's engine outside and walked toward the front window; the warmth of the sun beamed through the pane and jumped on my face.

The mailman stopped in front of our house and collected mail from a bin beside him in the truck.

Wow, he's early, I thought as he typically didn't arrive until about four. I opened the door and walked down the driveway. I flashed him a warm smile as he hurried his five-foot-three frame away to the next house.

Walking slowly back up the driveway, I opened up each envelope, shuffling past the "You could be a winner" and the "increase your car insurance" pieces of mail. We didn't get much mail because the post office hadn't forwarded everything yet. Reaching my hand out to open the front door, my eyes went to a letter that would ultimately be the beginning to the end of my marriage.

I stopped dead in my tracks. *Why am I receiving a letter from the rental office?* I opened the envelope, and big bold letters peeked their way out and took my breath away.

LATE NOTICE! EVICTION!

Those words stared up at me as if they were jumping off the page and slapping me in the face. I couldn't breathe, and my feet were blocks of cement. My body was cold even though the temperature outside was 80 degrees. Shaking and sweating, my hands grabbed the doorknob and I went inside the house.

We were being told to leave the house within two months. Tripping over the rug, I ran into the kitchen and picked up my phone to call Jason.

The blood pumping through my veins was hot as my body shook waiting for him to answer.

"Hey, babe," he said in a cool, calm voice. Hearing him pick up caused my voice to quiver. I was scared. *What do I say, what do I do? Oh my GOD this is crazy!* I thought. My mind was racing as I tried to find the words to speak.

"Hey," I said, my voice shaky. "There is an eviction notice in the mail today."

Before I knew it, I was crying. Tears flowed down my face uncontrollably and my breathing was heavy. Hyperventilating and wiping my eyes, I waited for his response.

"What... wait a minute, why?" His voice was calm. I couldn't figure out why he didn't react to what I had just said. I waited for a yell, a scream or something, but he was his normal calm self. Angry, I thought maybe he had people in front of him. He was at work when I called him, so maybe he didn't want to draw attention to himself.

"Jason, did you hear me?" I screamed. "What are we going to do? It says we have to leave in two months!" My eyes were red as the tears fell and smudged my eyeliner.

"I'll call you right back," he said. "We'll figure it out. Let me make some calls."

He ended the call. I sat on the sofa waiting for him to call me back, but he never did. Dusk dragged its ugly face through the living room window as the day started to end.

Two hours later and 10 unanswered calls to his phone, my phone finally beeped.

"Why didn't he call me?" Taking a long hard breath, I looked down and read the text message from Jason.

I'm sorry, you deserve better. I've messed up, and I tried but couldn't do it.

What the hell did that mean? I scrolled through the contact list and dialed Jason's number. Once again, it went to voice mail.

"I just can't believe this," I said. Shaking my head in disappointment, I sat on the sofa in shock. My body was numb, and my mind was flooded with worry. How could he do this to me? Did he leave me? Where is he? Why didn't he pay the rent? I couldn't understand what was going on. I didn't know what to do or who to call. Jason had a history of not paying bills on time, but this was different. This was my home. Just then, I got a chill up my spine, like someone had whispered into my ear: *Go upstairs.*

I stood up and ran upstairs and stopped in front of my bedroom door. My hands were clammy as I turned the knob and slowly waited to see what was on the other side of the door. A chill fell over my body as my eyes scanned the room. I felt like a stranger in my own bedroom. Still standing in the doorway, I reached down into my pocket and pulled out my phone, hoping he had called or text me, but he still hadn't. The room felt foreign and the walls were closing in on me. I couldn't believe my world was crumbling like this around me. Next to the bed was the closet door where he kept his clothes. Holding my breath, I slid the door open. I looked in and saw emptiness.

My eyes ran from corner to corner of the hollow closet. The breeze from the emptiness caused the hangers to rock from side to side. His pants were gone, his shirts were missing, and his shoes were MIA, too. Horror filled my eyes when I realized all traces of my husband were gone. He had taken everything. My only questions were how and why. At what point did he find the time to do this?

Moving away from the closet, I walked over to the nightstand next to Jason's side of the bed. Maybe I was wrong, I thought. He's not gone. Hope caused my heartbeat to slow up as I opened his drawer. Trying to catch my breath, my heart sunk and my head dropped as nothing but emptiness filled the space where his socks used to lie. I slammed the drawer shut and stood there, numb. I fell back on the bed and laughed uncontrollably.

I'm going crazy, I thought. "He left me here to get kicked out, that bastard!"

Dazed and helpless, I shook my head and walked back downstairs. Midway down the stairs, I stopped dead in my tracks. I was helpless. This man left me here and didn't care. The last years of our marriage rushed through my head. Walking down the rest of the steps, I stepped into the kitchen and rubbed my feet over the cool tile floors. I had just spent $300 on the tiles. I remembered going to the hardware store with Jason and picking out just the right color and style. We were both excited as we chose a neutral beige tile with a silver accent that meshed perfectly with the light brown paint on the walls and stainless steel knobs on the cabinets.

Confused, my freshly waxed eyebrows arched themselves. "If he knew he couldn't pay the rent, why did he let me pay for this dumb ass floor tile?"

I was so confused and didn't know what to think. My mind was exhausted and I couldn't think anymore. And to top it off, I still hadn't heard from Jason. Hours had passed and the clock on the wall inched its way to 7 p.m. Hungry, I paced around the house and still hadn't gotten my mind to focus. I picked up the phone, thinking I could get Jason to come home. Trying anything, I sent Jason a text. *Please call me so we can talk! Don't do this to me.* I had to figure out what the hell was happening to my marriage and to my husband.

I put my phone away and looked around the house. Staring at the walls in the hallway, I remembered telling Jason three weeks ago that I wanted to change the color. I imagined guests walking past the burgundy hues that lay over the oak chair rails. Last month, I had paid a handyman to come and put a backsplash behind the kitchen sink. All the time and money I put into this house and now my life was falling apart. I couldn't begin to understand what was going on. If he knew this was going to happen, why did he let me spend all this money? The more I walked around the house, the more agitated I became. I looked across the living room and at the garage door.

Maybe his things are just sitting in the garage, I thought. I wanted to have an excuse that this situation was not happening to me. I needed hope. Peeping my head into the garage, my eyes widened. The corner where he kept his baseball bat and gloves was empty; the boxes that held his certificates from college were gone.

"Ain't that a bitch?" I yelled. "I can't believe he left me! Damn."

I slammed the door and leaned against it.

I text Jason again, telling him that he needed to come back so I could figure out what to do next. I was angry, but I had to tell him everything was going to be ok and that we would work it out. I needed to say whatever I had to just to get him to come home. I needed him to face me like a man.

Waves of disgust washed over me because I had to do that, but it was a necessary evil. I needed to hear it from him in person. I needed to know what the hell was going on.

Two hours later and thirty unanswered texts later, he came home.

Laying on the sofa in the living room, my heart raced when the door opened. He walked in looking pitiful with his head hanging low. It was obvious that he had not been to work. With my hands on my hips, I stood up and stared at him.

"So where have you been?" Scared and tired from hours of waiting and wondering, I tried to stay calm and not yell. I needed to know what the hell had happened, and I didn't want him to run away again.

"I've been at the park."

"All day?" My high-pitched tone cracked with concern. I had to be dreaming, this was not real. Rubbing my chin in confusion, I sat down at the kitchen table and took a long hard breath. My leg shook rapidly as I waited for him to tell me why all his clothes were gone and why were we being kicked out of our house.

Jason stood there looking like a lost dog. I noticed the crisp white shirt he had ironed earlier was now replaced with a gray pullover wrinkled sweatshirt. The creased black dress pant with the one-inch cuffs was now old dirty gray sweatpants. Looking down at the floor with heavy brows and dark eyes, he didn't talk to me. Instead, his eyes shot from one end of the kitchen floor to the other as if the shame of what he'd done was weighing down on his head.

"I lost my job," he said with a low whisper. "I was embarrassed and I didn't know how to tell you."

My heart was breaking. Who was I to judge someone's bad luck? He was my husband, and I was supposed to stand by him. I would want someone to stand by me if I was down on my luck. My heart softened as I asked more questions.

"Where have you been going every day? I don't understand." I leaned in to look into his eyes.

After a long awkward silence, he raised his head and by the cracking of his voice, I knew this story was about to take its toll on my already tired mind. He began to take me back to three months ago. We were out having dinner at one of our favorite Italian restaurants. The whole time we sat there, he seemed preoccupied and antsy.

"Everything ok, Jason?" I knew he didn't seem to be his happy self.

"Yeah…we're good," he stuttered.

I still wondered what was up, but the ambience of the low music and dim lighting bouncing off one of the four chandeliers was breathtaking. My attention was caught. I splurged on a champagne colored dress with a Swarovski crystal neckline. I felt like a princess that night, but toward the end of our meal, Jason began to check his phone frequently. After two of his credit cards were declined, he decided to try his debit card. I knew the waitress was tired of walking back and forth to our table, but she smiled brightly each time she returned to say yet another card didn't go through. As we waited twenty minutes for the waitress to come back to our table the third time,

Jason was on the phone with his bank. I was embarrassed and knew something was going on.

"What do you mean you can't release my funds?" His eyebrows rose into his hairline as he argued with the person on the other end of the phone. I had never heard Jason raise his voice like that in public. Reaching into my purse, I pulled out my Visa credit card and motioned to the waitress. When she arrived, I handed her the card and paid for our dinner.

Frustrated, I stared at him. "You need to figure out what's going on with your bank, Jason. Now I have to change the bill pay this week until I get paid."

Shaking his head as if he couldn't understand what was happening, he spat out his words in disgust: "I can't stand this bank."

His eyes looked heavy as he stood up ready to leave the table. I should have known that there was something wrong back then, but I ignored it.

I tried not to blame myself for being so blind. I wanted to scream for him to leave and never talk to me again, but I stayed and listened.

Tears clung to his lashes and dropped on his shirt as he asked me to forgive him. I felt uneasy. My heart ached as he told me how embarrassed he was trying to find another job. My body was numb as I stared at him. Racing, my mind went back and forth deciding if I should stay with him. Could I just leave him like that? We hadn't been married that long. What would people think? Who was I to judge him? He was my husband, and I was supposed to stand by him. I would want someone to stand by me if I was down on my luck.

Something whispered in my ear, telling me not to leave.

Yes, he lied to me, but I decided to set some rules about paying bills so this would never happen again. Exhausted, I slowly rubbed my hands over my forehead and covered my mouth. Inhaling deeply, I sat down and stared at Jason. He looked sad and apologetic as he stood leaning against the kitchen counter.

I didn't have any more anger in me to yell, so I whispered, "I don't understand why you did this to me, but I love you, and we will work through this."

I stared down at the floor. I couldn't look at him. With his hands up ready to hug me, he walked toward me with a relieved look on his face.

My mouth opened as I looked at him. Something took over my body; as he moved closer,

I became stiff. Just as he reached down to touch my hand, I jumped away from him.

"You did this to me! Why? Don't you dare hug me!" I leaned against the wall and sobbed. He had ripped my heart out of my body, and I was sick with pain and hurt. With every breath, my chest tightened. Tears covered my face. I couldn't look at him. I wanted him to feel my pain. I needed him to hurt like I had been hurt. He never showed emotion, and this was the time for him to show it. Like a puppy with its tail tucked between his legs, he walked toward me and put his arms around me. Holding me tight like he was about to lose me, his hands were soft as were his words: "I'm sorry, I love you."

My resistance caved and my body felt like jelly. And in that moment, I felt like he really cared about me, so I sobbed. And as he held me tighter, I sobbed harder. Maybe he was *really* sorry about the lies he told. Maybe I was too hard on him. But just as my heart softened, my mind hardened and reality showed its ugly face in the room. Wiping my eyes with my shirt sleeve, I freed myself from his grip and gained my composure.

"I will not leave you, but we *will not* live together," I said as he looked at me and frowned. "Not right now. I'm selling everything in this house. You are going to move in with your mother, and I will be moving back to my parents' house."

Hanging on to every word, Jason stood there and nodded.

It was then that I felt I held all the cards in our relationship and he was powerless. I always gave Jason the benefit of the doubt that he was paying the bills on time, but when it came down to things that he cared about like buying baseball cards, I didn't care how he spent that portion of his money. I stood in front of him like a schoolteacher and gave him his test.

"From now on, you will communicate with me at all times. While we live apart, you will look for a new job and save your money. After a year of saving money, we will find another home and put our lives back together." I read off my demands to him like a drill sergeant. I was stern and I meant business. "Most important, you will *never* lie to me or hide anything else from me ever again."

Jason closed his eyes and took a long breath as if he was inhaling smoke from a cigarette. He looked back at me and softly nodded.

"And that means what?" I said, looking confused and mad at the same time.

"Yes, I agree with you."

"All right," I said as I walked away from him and into the family room. I sat on the sofa, drained.

I took a deep breath and let it out as I closed my eyes. I believed him and I accepted what was done. Why wouldn't I? He was my husband, and I married him for richer or for poorer.

Three weeks jumped into our lives so fast we didn't have time to think.

Jason slept on the sofa in the family room while I slept in our bed. We didn't talk too much, and he tiptoed around me so as not to upset me and concentrated on packing the rest of our belongings and taking them to storage while I went to work. Just like that, the house was empty. I had sold all that was worth something. The bed, the sofas, even the refrigerator was gone. What once felt like a comfortable home was now an empty complete stranger. My dream home was about to be gone, and there was nothing I could do about it. Taking the last walk through the house to make sure every piece of my life was gone, I couldn't help but think how sad my life had become and how I had lost the opportunity to enjoy the future in my home.

I stared into the backyard and thought about the barbecues we could have had. The Christmas parties we would have hosted.

"Are you ready?"

I blinked back tears as Jason's voice trailed off from inside the garage. His voice pulled me out of what could have been.

I turned around, grabbed my purse off the kitchen counter, and picked up the last box sitting on the floor. As if I was walking into a funeral, I hung my head down and walked slowly through the garage to the car Jason had been waiting in. Sitting in the car, I looked into my side mirror, back at our empty house. I could feel Jason looking at me, but I couldn't reciprocate the glance.

He started the car, and again I felt him looking my way. Out of the corner of my eye, I saw a half-smile come from him, but I still could not look at him. Holding in my tears, I stared down at my purse. I reached in and pulled out the letter that caused all this trouble. Pain moved around my stomach as the tears I held back made their way down my left cheek.

Jason cleared his throat, and I felt him turn away as those big black letters jumped off the page and frowned at him. I stared out the window at the house until it became a distant memory. Closing my eyes, I started to pray to myself as I gripped the letter in my hands.

I never believed a similar letter would destroy my world yet again only a few years later.

Chapter Three

Two years had passed since Jason and I left our dream home, and we were still living apart. I hated having to move back into my parents' home. I had been on my own for twelve years as an adult, so to move back in with my parents again was a complete letdown. The room I slept in as a child had since been turned into an office for my father. Instead of a bed, I slept on an uncomfortable futon, and my clothes stayed in boxes.

Although I was unhappy with my living arrangements, I knew this was what I had to do to get my life back on track. My heart was still broken, and some nights I sat on the futon, trying to figure out how this could happen to me and what would cause Jason to lie to me so much. Did I put too much pressure on him to live larger than we could? Maybe I overlooked all the signs of the issues he had because I didn't want to face them. I didn't know what to think. All I knew was that my husband was not with me, and my life was in turmoil.

I didn't let what happened to me affect my finances. I kept my head up and hid my pain. Work was my safe haven, so I worked just as hard and made sure my bills were paid on time. My parents were great about the living situation and didn't ask me to give them any money to stay with them. I didn't want to be a burden to them, so I made sure their refrigerator was fully stocked with food. I tried so hard to keep our separation a secret from my family and friends. I knew people were wondering when they came to visit my parents why I was there and Jason wasn't. Running out of lies to tell, I started to repeat the same story. It killed me to hide the truth.

"Jason? He's visiting his mother right now," I said when my uncle Matthew stopped by the house to visit my dad.

"I wanted to ask him a question about a baseball game," Uncle Matthew said, looking around the family room searching for traces of Jason.

Smiling nervously, I replied, "He'll be gone for a about an hour or two." I walked over to the TV and picked up the remote, hoping he would change the subject.

Walking around the mall even seemed to be a difficult task as someone was always asking about Jason's whereabouts. I was ashamed and embarrassed. Whenever I lied to others about where

Jason was, I wondered if they were talking about me and how long it would be before they found out the truth.

To keep the lies fresh, I made sure Jason and I were on the same page when people didn't see us together. I knew what lie to tell and made sure he remembered what to say. Even if I had to go to the bookstore by myself, he knew to tell people I was there. I didn't want anybody feeling bad for me. I didn't want anyone to know I had marital problems. I didn't want people talking behind my back, and I damn sure didn't want it to look like I couldn't make my marriage work.

Keeping secrets had become damaging to my health. I was nauseated all the time. Constant headaches and stomachaches had become a part of my daily routine, but I pushed through it.

To avoid the constant questions about Jason, I began to distance myself from my friends and family members. The judge had given me a life sentence, and my mind was in jail without parole. It would have helped to have a real friend who would listen to me and my issues without judgment, but at this point, I wasn't even sure who *I* was anymore.

Twice a day, I would talk to Jason. I would call him on my lunch break, and we would talk at night before I went to bed. His voice was always upbeat, and he seemed happier now that we were apart. He never complained and the stress of not having to take care of anyone else besides himself was freeing. We never discussed the topic of finding another home together unless I brought it up. He was content with our living arrangements. Because we both worked during the week, we only saw each other on Friday or Saturday nights. We would go out to the movies or to dinner. He would pick me up and would bring me back home before midnight as if we were teenagers.

Embarrassed at what he had done, he would sometimes sit outside in the car instead of coming in to get me. He didn't want to face my parents and couldn't find the right words to apologize to them for putting me in this situation. He was happy to pay for the dinners and sometimes purchased little gifts for me. He tried hard to make our situation seem as normal as possible. When we were at our old house, I never got gifts. So I was excited whenever he delivered one. I didn't even care what he gave me or where we went because we were together, and for a change, we were back to being happy. Or at least, it seemed like we were happy.

Figuring out the right things to say to me so that I wouldn't get upset, Jason avoided any and all conversations about money. One Saturday night before ending our normal call before bed, I asked him about a bill that we had to pay.

"Were you able to take care of that past due light bill from the old house that is on my credit report?" I made sure my voice was sweet and soft; I wanted him to feel comfortable telling me the truth.

Hesitating, he stumbled over his words. "Ummm, two weeks ago, I think," he said.

I took a long breath. I knew he hadn't paid the bill because I called the company that morning, and they said the payment was still past due.

"Hold on for a minute," I said. I dropped the phone on the bed and paced the bedroom floor.

"Here we go again," I said. "What the hell is wrong with him? Why is he telling me lies? I thought we were over this shit!"

Beating like a drum, my heart pounded through my chest. Each beat echoed through my ears, which caused my head to hurt. I massaged my temples and prayed to God for strength.

"Hello? Baby?" Jason's voice seeped through the phone and interrupted my prayer.

Shaking my head, I walked back over to the phone and placed it on my right ear.

"Yeah, I'm here." My tone was hard. "Are you sure you paid the bill?"

"Yeah." His tone went higher than his normal baritone I was used to. I couldn't stand it, and my head was about to explode.

"Why are you still lying to me?" I asked. My voice was harsh and strong. Not wanting to repeat history, he needed to know the frustration that was filling up my lungs. "You have no reason to lie to me! I know the bill is past due. Why are you lying?"

My breath was pushing through the phone like wind in a hurricane. Tapping my foot on the hardwood floor, I waited for his response. I could hear him breathe, but he remained quiet. I didn't even care about the bill anymore. I was so angry that he had lied to me again.

"Why are we doing this, Jason? This makes no sense. I can't keep doing this. If you keep lying to me, our marriage is over!"

While he remained quiet, I kept attacking. "We are in this situation because of you, and I refuse to let you bring me down." I had no idea if he was even listening to me, but I was so mad I just kept talking. "If you lie to me one more time, or if I find out that you are lying to me about anything else, it's over!"

Before I knew it, tears flowed down my cheeks, and my heart broke into pieces. This was not what I got married for. I wiped my tears with the inside of my shirt. In between short breaths, I managed to call out his name: "Jason? Jason, did you hear me?"

"I'm sorry…I was just trying to take care of it myself so you wouldn't have to worry."

The phone dropped from my hands and bounced on the carpet next to my feet. Staring down at the floor, I sat up on the bed and lay flat on my back. Staring at the wall, I was hurt and fed up. I didn't know what to do. I was the only one fighting for my marriage. I told him everything about my finances, and I didn't understand why he couldn't talk to me about everything. Even if I only had five cents in the bank, he knew about it.

I could not stop wondering why Jason kept things from me. I couldn't figure it out. What in the hell was wrong with him? Or was it me that was the problem? I couldn't remember a time when I made Jason feel like less of a man. I never questioned decisions he made or rebutted, but this lack of trust that entered our marriage had become a big issue.

"Lord, give me strength to help my marriage and to help Jason. Help me figure out why he is lying to me!" I screamed while tears streamed down my face. As night began to fall, I lay awake wondering why the Lord put me in this situation. Sleep crept up on me, and before I knew it, daylight peeked into my window.

Birds chirped as I blinked my eyes a few times realizing that I had fallen asleep crying. Just then Jason's name glowed under the sheets as Bobby Brown told Mr. Telephone Man something was wrong with his line. I set that ringtone for Jason's phone number because it was our favorite song. Looking down at the phone, I didn't even hear him say anything, but I immediately belted out my demands.

"I need you to find a counselor," I said. "You need help, and as your wife, I will go with you if you want." I waited for an answer, hoping this last-ditch effort to save my marriage would help him see that I loved him enough to stay with him throughout all of the issues we were having.

"Ok," he said quietly. "I will find a counselor." His words were short and quiet as a mouse. I smiled as relief ran through my stomach.

"Ok, I love you, and I'll call you tonight."

"I love you." His voice trailed off as if he was confused as to how the call ended. Maybe now, things would get better for us.

I got up to get dressed for work, and I felt good about what was about to happen for us and our fresh new start. Running my fingers across my forehead, I could feel the beat of a headache brewing. I hoped this would be the only conversation about counseling that Jason and I would have.

One month had passed, and Jason never brought up finding a counselor, and I never asked him about it again. Like sand slowly moving through an hourglass, I wondered, "Will we reconcile? Is Jason worth the time? Is there anything I can be doing to make this work?"

Time turned out to be my worst enemy, but I held on to the idea that my future would be brighter.

Chapter Four

Within a year, Jason had found a new job and was making good money as a supervisor for a janitorial company. I was able to catch up on a lot of my bills and was able to save some money, too. Nothing had changed in our relationship, but we were doing ok. We continued to stay connected, and he was communicating with me more. He told me everything that was going on with him financially and never left anything out. We were making it work, and I was looking forward to putting the pieces to the puzzle that was our marriage back together. We were getting along, and we were even able to go out of town to celebrate our wedding anniversary.

Despite the 180-change from Jason, I was cautious and alert and felt I would not be blind to what was going on around me this time. I wasn't completely happy with our living situations, but I was ok with the progression. I prayed constantly for him, and he became more active within our church community.

I always looked forward to attending church services with Jason. It was our time to connect spiritually once a week. His mother lived closer to the church, so we always met at the church and walked in together. It was important for me to keep up appearances because although we had told no one we were separated, we knew people were talking. Sunday morning as we stood talking in the parking lot, our pastor pulled in and parked next to us. Pastor Andrew was my favorite pastor. I had been a member of the Holy Light Temple Church since I was 13, and he was more like a father figure to me. Jason joined the church a year after we dated and had become a prominent member and male figure in the men's ministry for three years.

With a bright smile, Pastor Andrew put his Nissan Maxima into park and looked over at us. "Good morning, good morning," he said, moving quickly toward us.

In unison, we both beamed and responded, "Hi Pastor."

"How's everything going? Is everything ok?" As the three of us stood in the parking lot, I admired the pastor. You could see the genuine love for the Lord that was in his heart. He was wise beyond his 73 years and believed in marriage and was against divorce. He was soft spoken, and everyone knew he had an open door policy. Pastor Andrew was one of the few to know of our marital problems. Whenever he saw us, he made sure to tell us how prayer would help us.

"We're great, Pastor," Jason said before I could get a word out.

Rolling my eyes, I smiled and acted like there was nothing wrong. *We're not that great, but, ok*, I thought, hiding my real feelings.

Pastor waved as he flashed his warm smile toward us. "All right now, see you both inside."

Watching the pastor walk away, Jason turned and stared at me. A frown replaced my smile, and my eyebrows crossed each other.

"What did I do?" Jason asked.

I figured this was as good a time as any to bring up counseling. I hadn't spoken about it for a long time, and something told me to tell him how I felt.

"Well, I figured since we haven't met with a counselor yet, we can meet with the pastor just to get a better perspective of what's going on with us."

I crossed my arms and scanned the parking lot to make sure no one walking by could hear our conversation. We still had about 15 minutes before services started, so we didn't have to rush. I didn't want him to think I was jumping down his throat, so I softened my tone.

Gazing softly into his eyes, I stepped closer to him and took his hand into mine. Rubbing his fingers, I said, "I just want the best for us, that's all. Maybe Pastor can help us move faster to a resolution."

Agitation covered Jason's face, and I could tell he was bothered. "I'll think about it," he said, hunching his shoulders. "Let's go on inside."

Dropping my hands, he walked away. Looking at the back of his head, I took extra steps and moved quickly to keep up with him. The way things were moving in our separation, I avoided any potential arguments, and I didn't bring up counseling to him anymore.

Monday morning on my drive to work, I decided to call the church and set up an appointment with the pastor. If Jason didn't want to get counseling, I would go to get peace of mind for myself. Talking to my pastor always made me feel better, and I knew Pastor Andrew would help me spiritually.

Two weeks later on a Friday evening, I sat inside my pastor's study waiting for him to come in. His office was quiet. The peace in the room allowed my body to ease its tension and even if only for that moment, remove my mind from any negativity.

Memorabilia of the San Diego Chargers football team covered his office from wall to wall. My eyes moved around the room and took notice of every stuffed football, framed jersey, and team picture. He was a true fan and wanted everyone to know.

Sitting in the room, I felt comfortable. Faint sounds of the choir practicing down the hall for next Sunday's service could be heard. Rocking my head from side to side, I closed my eyes and listened to the organ playing. Different scenarios ran through my brain of what I would say to the pastor and what advice he would have for me. Shaking my head and blinking hard, I shook off the sudden nervousness and tried to find a peaceful thought.

"Why are you nervous, girl, this is Pastor Andrew. He knows your mom, your dad and your family, get it together."

Just then, with his warm smile, the pastor walked through the door.

"Hey, it's nice to see you!" He walked over to his desk and opened up a brown leather folder. Sitting in front of him, my eyes rolled over the large cherry wood desk. The top was layered in brown and gold marble and his leather chair was fit for a king. Pictures of his wife and three children happily adorned each corner of the desk. He was a family man. Something I had longed to have one day. Nestling into his seat, he showed all his teeth as he looked at me. I glanced over at the empty chair that Jason should have been sitting in and blinked. I don't know why I hid my meeting the pastor from him, but when I thought about what he had put me through with his lies, I didn't care anymore.

Shifting my weight and looking at the pastor, my words were awkward: "Well, Pastor, I just don't know what to say. Jason and I are moving along, but it's hard since we are still living apart. I think he is doing better financially, but I can only go by what he tells me. Other than that, we are happy."

Not knowing what to do with my hands, I pressed my thumbs against the purse that lie flat on my lap. I didn't want him to think I was uneasy. Two minutes had passed and he stared at his notebook.

Taking a deep breath, he digested my words, rubbed his chin, and leaned in to talk. "I had no idea you were still living apart from each other. If this relationship is what you both want, and if it is going to work, you have to find a place to stay together. You have to see each other, talk to each other, and be husband and wife." His words were matter of fact and stung like a bee.

I was embarrassed, but I nodded in agreement. He was right. I had become comfortable in my situation, and it had to change. It had been two years since we'd been separated, and there were no talks of us moving forward and finding a home together. It was time. If I wanted to continue with this man, I had to start moving forward. I had gotten used to living at my parents' house and having my own money again. I had gotten used to coming and going as I pleased and seeing him whenever I wanted to see him. It was like we were dating except we never had sex. I didn't even miss it. I never had a thought of being with my husband sexually. I needed to feel secure, and I didn't know how to ask for marital help. I needed the pastor to yell at me and tell me to get myself together, but he didn't.

Leaning back in his chair like a judge ready to give out a sentence, he spelled out what I needed to do and gave me a swift kick in the ass that I needed to move forward. "Find a house, an apartment, whatever you need to do and do it now," he said. "Your marriage will not work if you don't take action!"

My head hung low and touched my chest in shame. I traced the edges of leather on the bottom of my purse. Maybe I was afraid that Jason would continue to lie to me. Maybe I was afraid that he would lose his job again. I didn't want to struggle and be broke.

Biting my bottom lip, my mouth moved slowly as managed to get a few words out. "You're right. I'll talk to Jason tonight and get this started."

As I began to stand, I kept my gaze away from the pastor out of shame.

"It will be ok," he said. "Have faith and keep me updated." His voice was comforting and I was at ease. But, then again, he always made people feel good about any situation, good or bad.

The drive back to my parents' house was longer than normal. Usher was telling me his confessions through the radio. I was ready to attack my situation head on. I wanted to get my marriage on track with Jason. Selecting Bluetooth on my phone, I scanned through the call list and stopped at Jason's name. I was ready to tell him what was on my mind.

Jason answered on the first ring. "Hello?" he said, his voice low and raspy.

I stared at the phone, surprised. "Were you sleeping?" I asked, hoping he would say yes.

"No, just watching TV, what's up?"

I wasn't going to tell him that I had just left a meeting with the pastor and that I was still unsure about our marriage, so I lied.

"Nothing, I just left the grocery store. Listen, I need you to start helping me look for places for us to live." I paused, and when he didn't respond, I spoke louder. "What do you want to do, Jason? 'Cause if I'm going to continue living with my parents, then we do not need to be together."

Taking a long breath, Jason replied, "I agree. I'm tired of living here, and I want my wife back."

His response shocked me. My eyes filled with water, and the tears fell down my face. My throat tightened as Usher was about to finish confessing. Did I hear him right? Was he for real?

"Let's start looking tomorrow," he added.

The creases of my mouth widened as happiness burst through my smile. "I saw a

94

townhouse down the street from where we used to live if you want to look at it," I said. I was so happy that this was about to happen. We were about to move forward and be together again. Sure, I had doubts about Jason being able to tell the truth about things, but I had to trust him at some point. As long as we kept the lines of communication open, we would make it.

As I pulled into my parents' driveway, hesitation fell over my body like a chill. I didn't want to go in and sleep on that old futon tonight. Thoughts of snuggling under a soft white down comforter filled my mind as I walked into the house.

Just a little bit longer, I thought.

Saturday afternoon, we ventured out to look at houses. We had looked at houses before we were evicted from our first home, but this time it was different. Hope was riding in the car with me, and I had a good feeling this time.

Holding my hand and smiling at me as we made our way to the townhouse, Jason was upbeat and happy. It was these little things he would do that would remind me of why I married him. Pointing at a house we were about to pass, Jason looked over at me and slowed the car down.

Confused, I stared out the window. "What are you looking at?"

"Look at that yellow two-story house. It's for rent. Let's look inside."

I never thought about renting a house, not again, but as long as he was excited about us being together, I was game.

"Ok, stop the car."

Hopping out of the car, Jason walked around to my side and opened the door for me. Giggling at the thought of him being sweet, I stepped out smiling at him. We walked side by side up the driveway as the birds sang sweet songs.

As we walked through the house, Jason pointed out little things that needed to be fixed. He talked about the size of the rooms and what he imagined would go into each room. "We can put a sofa there. We can put a nice rug over here," Jason said as he quickly became attached to the house.

I nodded in agreement; it felt good to see him so involved. I, on the other hand, didn't show much expression. I didn't want to get my hopes up about the house until I knew we were going to be approved.

The real estate agent who had been greeting people as they walked through the house walked over to us.

"So what do you think?" she asked, smiling from ear to ear.

I frowned. I didn't know if I could take her seriously, not with the way she presented herself. A tan cowboy hat sat over her long stringy blond hair that barely fell over her ripped white T-shirt. Her tan linen shorts showed off her crisp brown tan. White lines between her toes matched the lines on her shoulders. Not what I would expect an agent to wear, but it was mid-June and 80 degrees outside.

"It's nice," I said with a half smile.

While I walked away to look at the fireplace, Jason asked her about some of the problems he saw with the windows and if some of the other issues would be fixed before we moved in.

"Of course, the owner himself will be here making the necessary adjustments before anyone moves in." She forced a crooked smile.

Jason looked over at me as to get my acceptance. Raising my eyebrows, I gave him a warm smile and a nod to let him know I wanted this house. "So what do we have to do?" Jason asked the realtor.

Reaching into a large brown fishnet purse that hung around her shoulders, she pulled out some papers and handed them to Jason. "After the credit check and your deposit, all you need to do is tell me when you are ready to move in."

I knew the credit check wouldn't be a problem for me because I had worked so hard at paying off all my debt. There was nothing on my credit report to hurt our chances from renting. Even though I hadn't seen any paperwork or documents proving that his financial issues were back on track, Jason never gave me a reason to think otherwise, so I figured his credit was on point, too.

"We'll get these back to you," he said, shaking her hand.

Back in the car, Jason and I took in deep breaths and looked at each other as we exhaled.

As if he had just won a baseball game 12-0, he smiled. "I like it," he said, searching my face for approval.

"Yes, I like it, too." I looked at the house as he started the car and pulled away. "The rental rate is great, and it's quiet out here." In my hands were the papers she had given to us. She told us to fill it out and fax it back to her by the following week with the deposit. We were supposed to go and see the house one more time, but we both realized this was the only house we wanted to see. The only problem we had was the deposit. Jason didn't get paid for another two weeks, and I didn't have enough to cover the entire deposit, so we waited and both agreed that he would pay the deposit when he got paid.

It had been two weeks since seeing the home, and I was anxiously waiting for an answer. Filled with excitement, I couldn't contain myself. I was on my lunch break when the message flew into my phone.

Hello. You were approved for the house and you can move in next month! Call me to set up a date to sign and pick up your keys! Mandy at Home Realty!

Wasting no time, I called Jason at work. I wanted him to hear the good news.

"Hey, what's up, baby?" he said.

"Guess what?" I yelled at the top of my lungs. "We got the house!"

In between his uncontrollable laughs, he managed to get out a few words to me. "I know. She called me ten minutes ago. I told her to text you, too."

For thirty minutes, we talked about the move-in date and where we would go to buy new furniture. We were starting from scratch. Spitting out ideas of what would happen next, I didn't give him a chance to tell me what he wanted to do to begin our new start.

"If you pay the house note, I will pay all the utilities. I think we can do it, Jason." He kept quiet as I kept advising. "Groceries we can split based on when we need stuff. Oh, and I saw this pretty sofa at the furniture store."

"Ok, ok, I got it, baby." His voice was agitated as he rushed me off the phone. "We'll talk about it after I get off work, I gotta go now."

Feeling awkward, a blank look covered my face. "Ok, I'll talk to you later then. Love you."

The phone went dead; he had disconnected before replying back to me. Was he upset with me? Maybe he was just busy. I couldn't figure out his tone. I wasn't going to let how he sounded take away my feelings of getting this house. It was going to be great. I'd leave my parents' house, move in, and finally be at home with my husband.

The day that we were supposed to sign the lease and pick up the key, I had to work and couldn't get the time off. Jason and I agreed that he would go at 11 a.m., and I would come by after I got off work. At noon, he called me.

"Did you get the key?" I asked, excited.

"No," he said. "They said that we have to pay a $100 pet deposit before we move in."

"Why didn't they tell us that before?" I asked, walking quickly into the break room at work. I didn't want anyone to hear my conversation. Tension in my head started to build up as my temples throbbed to a slow beat. *This is not going to happen*, I thought.

"Hold on," he said with a calming tone. "My mom said she would give me the money, but we just have to pay her back."

Thoughts raced through my mind as to what to say next. What was really going on? Is he telling me a lie? Why doesn't he have the money and why is his mother there?

"I'm about to go to the bank now and then I'll go to the office and pick up the key."

Taking a deep breath, I ran my hand over my mouth. "All right, just keep me informed."

"Once I take my mom to her doctor's appointment, I'll be on the way."

Before I could open my mouth, Jason hung up on me.

I sat in the break room as if someone had run over me with a truck. Things weren't adding up. He was supposed to go to the office early so we could get everything started. Here it was an hour after the fact, and he was driving his mom around. I was panicking.

*By the time he does all of that, the rental office will be close*d, I thought. Is he telling a lie again? My stomach was in knots, and I couldn't shake the feeling of something being wrong. I hoped he was not telling me a lie about the pet fee and his mother. I started to get a little angry. Why was his mother having him do all these things for her?

I knew they lived together, but knowing we had business to take care of today, why would he be running her around town? When we were first married, Jason and I decided to take a mini vacation to Las Vegas for the weekend. We were both doing ok financially, so we planned for a weekend stay. Neither one of us had been so we were both excited to travel. Jason mentioned the trip to his mother weeks prior to us leaving. The Friday we were set to leave on our flight, she became ill with a bad cold. And just like that, Jason cancelled our plans to make sure she would be ok. Of course I was livid. I knew she was faking because two days later, she was well enough to take a trip with her friends to a local casino, and she had no traces of sickness. Although I was upset, I didn't say anything to Jason about my frustrations. This was his mother, so I bit the bullet and remained quiet. As time passed in our marriage, frequent illnesses would arise when it was time for Jason and me to do something together. We rarely had days off together, but when we did we took advantage of them.

One cold winter Saturday in January, Jason and I decided to go on a road trip. Starting with breakfast, we would take a ride and do some shopping at the local mall and then see where the road took us. Anticipating a smooth day, I woke up and prepared myself for the day. Standing in the bathroom combing my hair and making last minute touch-ups to my makeup, Jason walked in the room and stood in the doorway.

Frowning, he held his cell phone up to his ear while shaking his head. I didn't know whom he was talking to, but I knew something was wrong. I searched his face for answers, but he looked down at the floor avoiding eye contact.

"Yeah, Mom. Ok, I'll be there."

The word mom was enough for my ears to start ringing. My lungs filled with air, and I let it out fast and deep. Placing the mirror back on the counter, I brushed past him so fast that I almost knocked him over. At the bed, I flopped down and began to untie my shoes.

Finishing his call, Jason turned and looked at me. His eyes followed down and up the length of me. "What is your problem?" he asked.

I stared at him like was crazy. The corners of my lips were wrinkled and my eyebrows were hanging down over my eyes. "I guess we are not going, huh? What's wrong with your mom this time?"

I didn't care if he didn't like my tone. I was tired of always being second to his mother.

"We're going, I just have to take her to the grocery store before we leave, that's all. Why are you being inconsiderate?" His tone was hard. I knew he was irritated, but was it toward his mother or me? "I'll be right back. We are going!" His words were convincing, but I didn't buy into it. I knew the routine.

Mrs. Jerry was in her seventies. She lived alone and didn't drive. She was a heavy smoker and sat home daily watching game shows and taking walks around her neighborhood. She couldn't drive and was dependent on Jason for everything. He was her personal grocery shopper, her driver, doctor appointment buddy, *and* son. I felt she took advantage of him, but I didn't want him to be upset with me if I talked about his mother, so I never told him how I felt. Even now, I felt she was making him drive her around town the day we were supposed to get the keys to our new house because she wanted to stop me from being with her son.

At four in the afternoon, I was sitting in my car on my lunch break. Not able to concentrate on the leftover fried chicken I made the night before, I waited for Jason to call me. Different scenarios ran though my head. Did he have to take his mother to the doctor? Were they at the grocery store shopping? The more I thought about what could have happened, the more worried I became. I didn't want to stop trusting my husband and I didn't want to drive myself crazy.

Reaching over to my glove box, I scanned the open CDs, searching for some stress relievers. My fingers ran over Deitrick Haddon's name, and I stopped. "Yes, I need some gospel right now."

Closing my eyes and nestling down into my leather seat, I listened to him tell me how great God is. Just then the buzzing of my cell phone rattled against the gearshift. Jumping up and grabbing it, I stared at the screen. It was Jason. Crossing my fingers and my legs, I put the phone against my ear and waited for the results.

Hesitating, I answered, "Hey."

"All right, I got the keys." His voice sounded like he had just won a race. Letting out a long breath, he sounded exhausted. "Mom and I are in the house and about to leave."

I kept my mouth shut and didn't ask him why his mother was there. I wanted to be the first one to open up the door with him. This was our new start. Instead of his wife, he experienced it with his mother. We had been through too much for me to

111

start an argument, and bringing up his mother

would ruin things, so I said nothing.

"That's good, baby," I said, sitting back in

my seat.

"I want to move in right now. I'll sleep on

the floor if I have to," he said, laughing.

I laughed out loud, too. "We got to get sofas

first. I'm not moving in with just a bed. We gotta

buy stuff, Jason."

With a sad tone, he gave in. "I'll take Mom

home, and I'll call you later."

Before I could say anything else, he hung

up. Suddenly, nervousness dropped into the pit of

my stomach. Maybe it was because I had been

living with my parents for two years and had

become settled. Maybe I wasn't ready to give up

having financial freedom every payday. Maybe I

was scared of what happened in the past. Whatever

it was, the feeling put my stomach in knots. I knew

I had to shake it off and get back to being a wife to

my husband.

Chapter Five

Three months after moving back in together, I had settled into our new home, and Jason was proving that he could be trusted again. Every two weeks I had to question him to make sure he was paying the bills on time. I hated treating him like a child, but I had to make sure that there was not a repeat of our first home eviction. We hadn't fully furnished each room, but that would come in time. I was content that we were now living together again as man and wife, and Jason was happy that he was in his own home again.

One afternoon in mid-August, I was just about to leave work and take a lunch break when my phone rang. Jason and I always talked when I went to lunch, so I wasn't surprised when I looked down and saw his name across the screen.

"Hey there, sexy," I answered, flashing a devilish smile. I laughed as I walked to my car.

His voice was uneasy, and he took short breaths as he spoke. "I think I lost my job."

I stopped dead in my tracks. My heart skipped two beats at a time as I tightened the grip on my phone. I could hear him talking, but I couldn't believe what he was saying to me. Holding my composure, I frowned and waited for him to continue with the bad news.

"They haven't put me on the schedule for the next two weeks, and I don't know why."

My breathing increased as I stood in the middle of the parking lot. I was worried, but I kept my tone calm; I didn't want him to hear me panic.

"Ok. Let's figure this out together. Have you called them? Did you speak to your manager first?" I asked.

Sadness took over his voice, and I could barely hear him. "I've tried to call them several times, but they are not calling me back."

"Why don't you go ahead and file for unemployment? Just in case something happens, your paperwork will already be in the system. We will be ok, baby." I didn't want him to panic like last time. I wanted him to know that I was there for him and that together, we would get through this hurdle. Most of all, I didn't want him to get scared and run. To show him I was going to work through this situation with him, I set up a plan to help us financially, just in case. Still standing in the parking lot, I finally made my way to my car and hopped in.

With my head sitting on the dashboard, I softly told him what I wanted to happen.

"This is what we're going to do, Jason. If you lose the job and get unemployment, you will still have income. Take three of those checks and pay the rent. Then with your fourth check, you can pay your car insurance and your car payment."

"Ok," he said with a dry tone.

"I'll continue to pay everything else, and if I need to, I will add money to supplement the rent."

We had come too far to fail, and I wasn't about to move back into my parents' house. He exhaled and his air came through the phone like he was in pain.

In a convincing tone, I said, "We'll be ok, babe, I promise."

Weeks and calls went by, and Jason still hadn't heard from his boss. Feelings in my gut told me he knew what was going on with his job, but he didn't want to tell me. I hoped for the best but prepared myself for the worse. Either way, I was going to be in control of the situation this time.

Three weeks and one income household later, we stretched the money I got paid from my job. Because Jason was receiving weekly unemployment checks, we were able to pay our bills on time. No more eating out, going to the movies and shopping. It was rough, but I was happy that we still had a house to live in and that we were together. Jason seemed to be in good spirits, but I could tell the situation was affecting him. His weight had dropped from 250 pounds to 145 pounds. I thought it was because we were eating lighter than normal. When I questioned him, he

118

would always say he didn't know why he was losing weight.

Smiling, he would always joke about his stomach: "Maybe now I can see the six-pack abs I've always wanted."

Instead of his normal size 3x shirts, he wore a scrawny extra large. His belts hung extra low on his pants and were now reaching the last hole in the line. I was so busy working that I had no idea that he was wasting away before my eyes.

Jason seemed to be ok with staying home and sleeping the days away. When I came home, he was either still sleeping or just getting up. It was a strain on our relationship, and I became irritated that he did nothing all day but sleep, but we continued on.

Finally, after weeks of searching for a job, Jason received a new janitorial job. He was ecstatic to be working and making money again, and I was happy to have the financial load off my shoulders. Knowing the first few paychecks would have low hours because of training, I kept Jason under a watchful eye to make sure our bills didn't fall behind. I regularly asked for receipts that the rent was being paid. He began to get agitated with me when I asked, which was understandable, but his track record caused me to micro-manage him at all times. Jason worked overnight shifts, and I worked during the day, so we hardly saw each other.

After a long day of working, I came home and immediately went to the kitchen to get the mail. Preparing himself to go to work, Jason walked into the kitchen yawning. His frail body hid under the dark blue pants and matching button down shirt he wore, and his eyes were dark from sleeping all day.

Our normal "Hi" and "See you later" were just about as much of conversation that we had.

Looking out the corner of my eye as I shuffled through the bills, I noticed him walking slower than normal. "What's wrong?"

"They messed up my check again," he said, staring down at the floor.

Confused, I laid the mail down on the kitchen table and sat down. Bracing myself for the bad news, I crossed my arms and waited.

"They shorted me eight hours again. And when I call the payroll person, they never call me back."

I didn't speak a word. Heat from my face started rising, and I stared at him with cold eyes. Taking a gulp, I quietly found the words to speak. "Did you tell your supervisor? Doesn't he put the time in?"

"Yeah and he told me he would look into it."

This angered me. I couldn't understand why he never told me this before. Just then something clicked in my brain as to what he just said. I tightened my eyes as if I couldn't see and scrunched up my nose and mouth like a rabbit.

"Wait, what do you mean *again*? How? If it was my paycheck that was short more than once, I would be in someone's office making a complaint!" I yelled at him like he was a teenager that knew better. But he wasn't a teenager. He was my grown ass husband.

He brushed me and the situation off like we weren't important. Rushing out the room, he said, "Look, I'll take care of it. The bills will get paid." The irritation in his face told me he was avoiding the situation, *and* he was hiding something.

Damn! Here we go again. He better not cause me to lose this house, I thought.

Because I didn't trust him, I continuously asked Jason about his pay. When I asked if he had called his human resources office to fix the paycheck issue, his answer would be the same: "No, not yet." I was all too familiar with this answer. It was the same answer he gave me at our previous house when I would ask him if the bills were being paid. I knew something was going on, but I didn't know what. I knew he was telling me lies, but I didn't want to lose the house I had worked so hard to get into, so I continued to put my feelings to the side and not say anything to him. I had no proof of any wrongdoing, so I concentrated on making sure I kept a roof over my head by working even harder to make money.

One night when I came home from work, I walked in the bedroom and found him asleep in the La-Z-Boy chair beside the bed. He had gray sweatpants on and a white tank top. Sometimes, I would just peek in the room to tell him that I was home, and then go get something to eat in the kitchen. But this time I noticed something different about him. I had seen him sleep before, but this time, I was stuck watching him. This was the first time that I had *really* looked at my husband in a few months, and I was shocked at what I was seeing. He lay on his side with his hands tucked under his face. He was sleeping in the fetal position. His skin looked as if it was hanging off the bones. I stared at him and couldn't stop staring. I found myself leaning against the wall just shaking my head in amazement. He was skinny. He had lost so much weight that it scared me. He looked as if he was about 90 pounds. He looked smaller than me, and I was about one hundred thirty pounds. He looked like he was sick, and I couldn't believe what I was seeing.

How in the world had he lost so much weight and I not notice it? Did I lose that much interest in my husband that I didn't even notice that he was wasting away? I stood there in the doorway trying to figure out how this had happened, and what had caused his drastic weight loss. I realized that whenever he was around me or whenever we went out, he dressed in layers. Most men wear a shirt under their main shirt anyway, so I guess I never paid attention to him. I realized that I was so worried about making money and paying bills that I didn't have time to notice that my husband was wasting away. I was worried and didn't know what to do.

125

He opened his eyes and looked over to see me watching him. He stretched and in between yawns managed to squeeze out a "Hey."

I walked closer to him and sat down on the bed.

"I'm worried about you," I said, trying not to look like I was scared.

"Why?" He stretched and yawned again.

"You have lost so much weight. Why? What is going on?"

"I don't know. Maybe I'm working too much. I guess it's just stress."

Not knowing how to react or what to believe, I blurted out something I knew he would disagree to: "Maybe you should see a doctor, just to make sure nothing is wrong." I knew he hated going to the doctor's office, and I couldn't remember him ever going for checkups.

126

Pushing himself out of the chair, he stood up and growled at me, "I'll make an appointment when I get ready." He stormed into the connecting bathroom, slamming the door behind him. I jumped as the sound echoed through the room. A feeling of awkwardness fell over me, and I became confused at his reaction. I didn't want to argue with him, so I left the room and walked downstairs to the guest bathroom. Turning on the faucet to wash my hands, I stared at myself in the mirror. As I scanned over the frown lines that had permanently made a home in my forehead, I shook my head. I hated how the stress of my relationship with Jason was causing me to look older than I really was. After drying my hands, I walked over to the sofa and turned on the TV.

Thirty minutes later, a dressed Jason hurried down the stairs ready to leave for work. Sitting on

the sofa holding the remote, I looked up at him.
Scared at another bad reaction, I was hesitant to say
anything, but I blurted out something that would
cause him to look at me with hate in his eyes: "Are
you on drugs?" Then I grinned at him so that he
would think I was joking.

Turning and looking back at me, the look he
gave me pierced through my heart.

"I'm just joking!" I said, laughing so that he
wouldn't take it personal. I had to make sure he
didn't fly off the handle. No one wants to be called
a drug addict.

With a short chuckle, his frown softened as
he shook his head and grabbed his blue square
lunch bag.

"Bye," he said, throwing it over his left
shoulder and slowly closing the door behind him.

Happy to avoid an argument, I took a long breath and closed my eyes. I experienced family members using drugs, so I knew the symptoms of alcoholics and drug users. I hadn't seen any "crackish" ways, and there were no items or money missing from the house, so I let the thought go.

Time went on and things between Jason and I remained the same. Our relationship wasn't as great as it should be, but because I was so engrossed with working and paying the bills, I hardly paid any attention to my husband. He never asked to go out to eat or to a movie, and we stopped going out on dates all together. We only had sex about once a month, and I never wanted to participate. When we first met, we would watch movies together and snuggle on the sofa. Now, he sat alone in the bedroom and watched TV while I sat alone in the family room. Dinner was always ready when I came home from work, but we ate in separate rooms. The bedroom had become his hideout, and I didn't care anymore. Sometimes, I would try to get him to come downstairs and watch a TV show with me, but he would always say he didn't like the show that I was watching and go back into the bedroom. We were growing apart fast and even Jason's appearance deteriorated.

One Saturday afternoon in May, we were waiting around for the maintenance man to fix a leaky toilet in the guest bathroom. It was about 80 degrees outside and unseasonably warm. People outside were wearing shorts, and we even had the windows open. I was downstairs in the family room hanging a few pictures I had just purchased from the art store down the street from our house. Jason was upstairs in our loft watching TV, and because I hadn't paid too much attention to him, I hadn't noticed how he was dressed. Just as I finished

hanging the last picture, the doorbell rang.

Jason rushed past me to open the door. "I

got it," he said as he grabbed the doorknob.

Standing there waiting for the door to open,

my left eyebrow raised and my lips parted. I looked

at Jason and shook my head in embarrassment.

"What in the world is he wearing?" I whispered to

myself. He had on a pair of gray sweatpants and

two T-shirts. On top of his clothes, he had on a

wool knee length robe that I bought him for

Christmas last year. Around his neck was a towel.

He looked as if he was just about to step into a

boxing ring. Turning away and walking into the

kitchen, I was not only embarrassed for the man

who had come to fix the toilet, but I was

embarrassed for my husband.

Sitting at the kitchen table with my head in my hands, I waited for the maintenance man to start working. The sound of footsteps could be heard moving down the stairs. Whistling like he didn't have a care in the world, Jason walked into the kitchen and opened up the refrigerator door. Bent over, searching for something inside, he ignored me.

Raising my head, I looked over at him and contemplated what I would say to him. I cleared my throat and hoped for an easy conversation. "Why are you dressed like that, Jason?" I asked.

Of course he didn't give me the answer I was hoping for. "What?" he said as if he was dressed like a normal person.

I pointed toward the kitchen window as a warm breeze came through and pushed the lace curtains up and down off the window seal. "It's so warm outside, and you are wearing all of that like it's cold outside."

As if he didn't care, he looked at me and frowned. "I don't care, I'm comfortable."

I couldn't believe he thought that the way he was dressed was ok. I thought he was crazy and felt I was going crazy.

"Well, you look weird."

Grabbing a soda, he turned away and walked out of the kitchen. He made no eye contact with me as he turned away and went back upstairs. I sat at the kitchen table not knowing what to think. I had gotten tired of trying to figure him out and continued to go through the motions.

Chapter Six

Time went on, and our marriage had become non-existent. I tried to figure out a way to bring us a little closer and change things. I was happy that Jason was able to get his work schedule changed to days instead of nights. We still didn't go out together, but we were able to see each other more often.

One Saturday afternoon, as I cleaned the family room, I noticed the mailman had arrived early. Usually, I was at work, or running errands when he arrived at four o'clock, but today he arrived three hours early.

Walking over to the desk sitting by the front door, I decided to call Jason to see how his workday was going. He didn't get off work until five, so he had about four more hours to go. I looked through my purse and shuffled through the money I had tucked away for a bill. I counted to see if I could spare enough to take him out to dinner just so we could have a change in scenery. His mother lived about 20 minutes from his job, and sometimes after work, he would go there first to see her before coming home. I knew I had to get to him first so I could tell him my plans because if not, he would probably make plans to see her when he got off.

It was nice outside, so I decided to talk to him while I sat on the front porch. When I called him, he picked up on the first ring, which meant he was not busy.

"Hey, what's up?" he asked, sounding upbeat.

Matching his tone, I smiled. "Not much, just calling to see how work is going."

I could hear cars driving by in the background, so I figured he was on a break and standing outside. Standing up, I walked over to the mailbox to get the mail. The warm air blew into the phone as Jason asked me if we had hamburgers in the freezer.

"I think I'll cook on the grill tonight," he said. "We haven't done that in a while."

"Yeah, we do, but I was thinking we could go out to eat tonight," I said, opening the mailbox lid. Pulling out the mail, I turned to walk back toward the house. Distracted while I flipped through each piece of mail, I half-listened as Jason went on about what happened to a co-worker earlier. My eyes were stuck on a letter from our rental office. *JC Smith And Company* covered the

front envelope in black handwritten letters in a
small white envelope.

Slowly walking up the walkway to the front
porch, I blinked twice as Jason yelled at me. "Did
you hear me?"

"Uh, yeah," I said. I couldn't say another
word as my throat clenched.

"What's wrong?" he asked.

Sitting on the brick steps, I stared down at
the envelope. My stomach started to turn as I tried
not getting upset right away. It could have been a
routine letter from them. There were times they
sent us letters to let us know that we could
schedule a maintenance walk-through for the items
we marked off during our initial walk-through.

"Why would the rental office be writing to
us?" I asked.

Without any hesitation, he responded, "I don't know."

My chest moved up and down as my breathing increased. Nervous and scared of what was inside the letter, I started to have flashbacks of our past eviction. My hands were clammy with sweat, and the warm air blowing around didn't help. I stood up and walked back into the house and sat on the sofa in the family room. I looked up, and the blades from the ceiling fan put me in a trance and took me back to being kicked out of our home two years ago. Running my hands over the letter, I realized Jason was too quiet and knew what was going on. Still holding the phone against my ear, I used my shoulder to position it against my face.

Lies From His Heart | Shelby Britt

It's too thin to be an eviction notice, I

thought. Pulling out the one page letter, my heart

began to beat like a drum.

"I have to go," Jason said. "My boss is

calling me." Nervousness took control of his voice

and the rest of the call. I knew he didn't want to be

on the phone when I opened up the letter, so I

stalled him.

"Wait." I unfolded the paper, but he had

already hung up. Angry, I sat the phone down on

the sofa next to me. The letter was folded into three

sections. Reaching the last section, I took a breath

and gulped. My hands shook as my eyes scanned

over the white piece of paper. Déjà vu had entered

my house, and I started to have an out-of-body

experience. I dropped the letter and watched it sail

to the floor. My body slid to the floor and

trembled.

139

"No. This is not happening to me again!"

My breathing was long and heavy this time like a panic attack. I could not believe what I was seeing on the paper. I looked over at the letter sitting comfortably on the carpet. Maybe I read it wrong. Maybe the sunlight hit the letters too hard, and I misread what it said. Reaching for the phone, I called Jason back, but he didn't answer. The call went straight to voice mail. I picked up the letter again and stared at it. *LATE NOTICE, THIRD ATTEMPT* was in big black letters across the top of the page. Hyperventilating, I put my hand on my forehead and the other hand on the paper. *You have 10 days to make a payment to avoid court notification.* I couldn't believe he had done this to me again.

"Why? Why? Why?" I said. The tears were not falling, but my body was numb. I called him again, and he answered. I heard him answer, but I don't know what he said. My fear took over my voice. I begged him for answers. "How could this happen? Why didn't you pay the rent? What in the world is going on, Jason?" My anger level was on 100, and I was ready to spit fire.

In a calm voice, he answered, "I paid the rent. I don't know what they are talking about, I need to call them."

"Stop lying to me," I screamed until my voice cracked. "I've had enough, just tell me the truth. For once, just talk to me!" I pleaded.

He couldn't do it. He was caught. He couldn't even tell me the truth. "Look, I got rounds to do, and I'll call you right back."

I wasn't even surprised when he hung up. When times got rough, he always found a way to disconnect.

Looking down at my phone, I searched through my contact list. Scrolling through, I stopped at the one name I could trust. This person was always there for me, and I knew he would be there for me again. Tapping the screen, I waited for him to answer my call.

As soon as I heard his voice, I broke down crying.

After telling my father about my conversation with Jason and the eviction letter we received, I knew my dad was the only person who would help me figure things out. He always put his needs aside and turned every bad situation into a good situation. I was his only girl, so whatever happened in my life, he was always there for me, financially and mentally. I was independent, so I never burdened my dad with the worries I had with Jason. Whenever I did need to talk to him, which

142

was not too often, he never judged me and that I

loved about him. When Jason and I separated years

ago, my father never commented. He didn't get

angry or criticize Jason. He let me know that he

was there for me and would help out in any way

that he could. This time was no different. Sniffing,

I wiped my face with a mound of used tissues

sitting in my lap. My breath was short and quick,

but I managed to get the words out to tell him what

happened.

"Hey Dad, Jason didn't pay the rent this

month, and we are being evicted if we don't come

up with $1,000. I don't know what to do. I just

can't do this anymore."

The tension in my throat tightened as the

tears started to fall again. What sounded like words

to him were minutes of mumbles to me.

Calm as usual, he finally spoke. "Well, baby," he said, taking a long breath and letting it out. "I can't tell you what to do with your relationship, but I will help you pay the bill. There is no way I will let you be evicted again. I thought Jason had a job now and everything was ok." Concern poured from his voice. I was at a loss of words. Shame covered my body, so I couldn't bring myself to tell him how bad of a time we were having.

"He is working, but," my voice trailed off, "I guess he isn't making enough. I don't know what to say. I guess he got behind. It's too much, Dad." I wanted to curl up into a fetal position and hide from the embarrassment.

"Ok, I'm listening," he said.

"Dad, I'm tired of working so hard just to keep losing everything because he is not good with

144

money." Holding my breath, I could hear him thinking through the phone.

When he spoke, his words were direct and strong. His tone was a mixture of Barry White and Don Cornelius, which calmed my nerves. "Stop crying, baby, it'll be ok. Come over to the house tomorrow and pick up the money."

And that was it. He had nothing else to say. He was a man of few words.

"Ok, thanks, Dad. Love you."

"Love you, too, hon."

Any other person would be relieved, but I didn't feel relief. The fear of being evicted was gone, but the pinch of dealing with my missing in action husband was still stabbing me in my side. Falling back on the sofa, I exhaled and tried a few more times to call Jason. No answer. I gave up and

145

collected defeat. Then the wheels in my mind started to turn. And I was stronger.

I didn't want to deal with his lies about what happened to his paycheck, and I didn't want to see another eviction notice. And I shouldn't have to. I didn't want to hear his sad stories about loving me and wanting better, and I didn't want to lecture him on communicating with me. And I shouldn't have to. I deserved more. I didn't want to go back to acting like everything was ok to the outside world. I was faking like I had a good marriage when the truth was it was over a long time ago because of lies.

In Jason's mind, he told me the truth, but his heart told me lies.

I looked at the clock on the cable box and realized an hour had passed since talking to Jason. Just then, my phone beeped. Looking down out of the corner of my eyes, I saw Jason's name blink on the screen. Instead of calling me and being honest, he went the safe route and sent me a text message.

I'm sorry I keep messing up. Maybe you will be better off with someone who can be and do better. I tried to handle things myself, but I keep messing up.

I deleted the message. I was not in the mood to give him any pity, and I was not going to fall for the "I don't know what happened" story again.

"How did I even last this long in this relationship?" I asked. Picking up my phone, I dialed his number. I didn't know what I was going to say. I was hoping that for once, he would be honest with me, but honesty had flown out the window years ago along with our marriage.

In a low, quiet tone, he answered the phone as if he was waiting for me to unleash a can of whoop ass on him. But I didn't and I didn't give him an opportunity to speak either.

"Please tell me the truth," I pleaded with him. "Tell me why we are back in this place again. Please tell me what you are doing with your money." I couldn't believe I was speaking to him nicely. I should have been yelling, but I didn't have any more strength to yell. I threw it all at him and waited for a small glimpse of the truth to come out of his mouth.

After all he put me through, I still hoped for a silver lining.

"I said I'm sorry," he said. "What else can I do?"

That was all he could say?

I was trying not to talk loud and raise my voice, but I lost it. Heat rose from my neck, and my eyes were popping out of my head.

"You might as well just come home and write the word fool on my forehead because that's exactly how I feel right now!" I yelled. "This is my life and I chose it."

"What?" he asked. "What does that even mean?"

"You heard me! I can't do this no more, this is just so…so ridiculous that I have to keep going through this with you!"

I panted heavy like a dog. Hot tears streamed down my face and dropped on my white T-shirt. Thinking he hung up on me again, I took the phone away from ear and looked down at the screen. I heard him breathing, but he said nothing. "So you are not going to say anything?"

"I got rounds to do," he said with a short tone.

"Well that is not enough. I need an answer now."

The line went dead.

Pissed and beyond upset, I yelled at myself, "Did I sign up for this treatment?" I called him back two more times, and his phone went straight to voice mail. Hours went by that night, and I soon realized that not only was he not going to call me back, but he was not coming home.

At eleven-thirty, I put my pajamas on and climbed into the king size, pillow top bed we had purchased before we moved into the house. Pressing my hands side to side against the comforter as if I was testing it out at the store, I thought about how it seemed so big now that he would not be sleeping on it. I looked down at my left hand and noticed the difference in skin color.

The area where my wedding ring used to sit was

lighter than my normal skin color. My ring finger

was empty because I had given it back to Jason

until he understood the meaning of being married. I

stared at the floor and realized I would probably

never see my wedding ring again. Rubbing my

hands over my empty ring finger, I thought back to

the day that I took my ring off.

Six months ago, Jason and I were sitting in

the family room watching TV. I was on my laptop

looking at bills, and he had just nodded off. I

realized I needed a pen to write something down,

so I got up and went into the kitchen. I was not

able to find a pen anywhere.

While looking over pieces of paper on the

kitchen table, I noticed Jason's blue members only

jacket hanging on the chair. I knew that he always

kept a pen in his jacket, so I walked over to check. As I reached into his top pocket, I was shocked at what I saw. I reached in and pulled out the white box with green trim. It was a pack of cigarettes. I cringed when I read the word *Newport.* He had lied to me so many times before, so I shouldn't have been surprised this time. Years ago when I met Jason, he smoked. I told him of my dislike for cigarettes. I told him stories of how my step-grandfather passed away from lung cancer. I told him of my cousin who had throat cancer. And I told him of how both of my grandparents smoked till they passed away. I loathed the smell of smoke, and I didn't want to be in a relationship with anyone who smoked. He said he understood and would quit. Because his mother smoked so much, I knew there was a chance that he would succumb to the urges. I mean, if he was around her every day, of course he was going to have the urge to smoke.

However, he said he would never smoke again, and

I believed him. Just like I believed everything else

he said. Every sign about Jason was right in front

of my face, but I overlooked them.

There were times when I would get into his

car, and it would smell like air freshener. I had no

idea that he was spraying it down before I got in to

cover up the toxic smell of smoke. He would

always say that his mother was smoking in his car

when he took her to the store. I gave him a look as

if to say you are not telling me the truth, but I

dared not question him about his mother. I felt I

was overstepping my boundaries if I did, as

always.

"You are not smoking again, are you?" I

would ask him. "No." No was always his answer to

my questions. "I don't even like the smell of it anymore."

So as I stood in the kitchen staring at the pack of cigarettes that my husband had hidden in the top pocket of his jacket, all I could say to myself was "What a liar."

I walked over to the door of the kitchen and looked at my husband sleeping. I was disgusted. Still holding the cigarettes, I walked over and stood in front of him. He was still asleep and didn't feel me standing over him. Looking down at his face, my eyes zoned in on his lips, dark gray and cracked; they were classic smoker's lips. Every person *I* knew who smoked heavily had dark lips. I didn't even know he was smoking, and now that I knew, I could prove it.

The evidence was in the palm of my hands. There was no way he could lie to me this time.

154

Thinking of what I would say to him when he woke up, I braced myself for his reaction. Making sure I didn't wake him, I tiptoed around the room setting up the scene. Picking up the cigarette box, I lay them right next to his face so that when he opened up his eyes the evidence would be staring right back at him. Quiet as a mouse, I sat down in the chair next to him and waited. Anxious and fidgeting in my seat, I picked up my laptop and sat it on the coffee table in front of me making sure to make a noise.

His eyes popped open, and I saw him blink to focus on the white box with the green stripes in front of his eyes. He lifted his head and looked at me.

"What's that?" I asked. He looked over at the box and looked back at me.

"I don't know."

"What do you mean, you don't know?"

Gritting my teeth, I took a breath and glared over at him. Then the lies started rolling in. And as the lies rolled off his tongue with the greatest of ease, I sat there and rolled my eyes along with him. I rolled my eyes so much my eyeballs were sore.

"They are not mine," he said. "I found them. They're my mother's."

He didn't even care that I wasn't falling for his lies. The more excuses he gave, the angrier I became. Before I knew it, I stood up and screamed. Screaming so loud, I started to shake. "Enough! You can't tell me the truth to save your life!"

Staring at the floor, he was at a loss for words. He hung his head and his chin touched his chest. Placing both hands on my hips, I looked down at my ring ringer. A bell rung in my brain, telling me what I needed to do next. He needed to know how serious I was. I reached over to my ring finger, slid off my wedding ring, and held it in the air in front of his face.

"Here," I said. "You take this ring and keep it." He reached out his hand and took it, still looking like he had done nothing wrong. "Until you feel like I am wife enough for you to tell me the truth and communicate with me, I don't want them back. Obviously you don't consider me your wife because you keep lying to me."

"That's not true," he said as he dropped the ring into his pocket and walked out of the room. I was overwhelmed with grief because he didn't put up a fight to give it back to me. I was hurting, and he didn't care. Maybe he didn't want to be married. Maybe he was acting out so I would leave him. Or maybe seeing the wedding ring off my finger would make him get his act together.

"What did I just do?" I asked myself. I was so quick to take off my ring that I didn't realize what people would think. I didn't realize someone would notice my missing ring and question me. "Damn, what now?"

Walking over to my purse sitting on the floor, I reached in and pulled out a piece of gum. As I sat down on the sofa, I stared off in a trance figuring out my next move. "Yeah, that's what I'll say," I whispered to myself. "If anyone asks, I'll tell people that my ring is being cleaned." In my mind, I had won half the battle. The reality was that I would never win the race, or see my wedding ring again.

I didn't get much sleep. Tossing and turning throughout the night, my mind wandered like a lost puppy. My marriage was over. Jason making the decision not to come home sealed his fate in ending our relationship. Because my thoughts were all over the place, I didn't realize that I finally drifted off to sleep until my alarm clock went off.

Pounding through my ears like cymbals, the sound of the alarm clock rose higher and higher until I reached over and slammed my hands across the top, hitting every button. The clocked flashed 7:00 a.m., one hour before church service, and I knew I was not in the mood for church, so I remained still.

I stared up at the ceiling and then looked over at the empty pillow next to me. Even though he lied, Jason was a smart man. I knew he was going to come home if I left. Fearing he would pack all of his things like he did at our old house and leave, I decided to beat him to the punch and wait for him to come home. I was going to give him what he wanted, out of this relationship. Then I realized that I was also giving myself what I was wanting for years. I was giving myself the confidence to get out of a relationship that I had been miserable in for so long. This was the day, and now was the time.

Pushing myself out of the bed with my newfound strength, I got up and prepared myself for the rest of my life. Ever since I was little, I waited to get married and find the man of my dreams. Problem was, I thought I had finally found my Prince Charming, but what I really found was a box of happily never after.

Chapter Seven

One week after Jason walked out, I took a much-needed vacation from work. To clear my mind, the first thing I needed to do was get my house in order. I needed to clean the house and rid all traces of our marriage out of the house and my mind.

Awkwardness fell over my body when I walked into the bedroom Jason and I used to share. It wasn't *our* room anymore. I wanted it to be *my* room. My eyes scanned over the room and stopped on the chair. Burgundy in color, the arms and headrest were worn and dingy. He never slept in the bed, so the chair became his sanctuary and the room was his hideout. He woke up in the morning and ate breakfast in that chair. He would watch TV and eat dinner in that chair. And because I was a light sleeper, he slept in that chair. The slightest move from him would wake me up. There were some nights when all I did was push him and shake him to turn over because he would snore. When Jason snored, I would wake him up, and he would go and lay in the chair. This went on for years. I don't think I ever got a decent night's sleep until he started sleeping in the chair. I'm sure he hated it, but he never said anything to me.

I still remember the day I purchased the chair. I decided one afternoon to go to a furniture store to look for a new sofa for the living room. As I walked through the bedding area and into the living room area of the store, my eyes stopped on the recliners.

"These are nice," I said as I rubbed my hands up and down the soft microfiber headrest.

Jason had a habit of sitting and eating on the bed, so I knew this would be perfect for him. It was a La-Z-Boy made of soft microfiber material and was just the right size for him to get comfortable in. I was excited to pay for it and have it delivered. I wanted it to be a surprise for Jason. At the time, he was trying to communicate with me and rebuild our relationship, so this was a perfect gift for him. As time went on, I began to hate that chair. Instead of sitting next to me watching TV or eating dinner at the kitchen table with me, he sat in the La-Z-Boy.

I rolled my eyes and walked over to the closet door. Reaching in, I pulled out the vacuum cleaner. Unwinding the long black cord, I plugged it into the wall, hit the switch and began to move it around the floor. Detaching the hose from the side compartment, I walked over to the chair and began to work. I needed that chair to be clean. I pushed it through all of the creases of the chair. Putting my hands on my hips, I looked around and searched for the fabric spray I purchased days ago. I took the fabric spray and sprayed the entire chair until it was completely wet. I wanted it to smell different now that Jason was gone. Making sure no dry spots were left, I ran my fingers across the back of the chair to make sure it had been covered, too. Next were the floors. I took the vacuum and ran it up and down his side of the room. I took the dusting spray and a white terry cloth and wiped over the nightstand next to his bed. I changed the sheets and pillowcases and put on a clean comforter. Working up a sweat, I was on a mission to clean myself of the present situation.

I walked over to the TV and looked above the screen. Hanging two inches above it was our wedding portrait. Standing on the tips of my toes, I moved it off the nails and sat it on the floor. Looking at the empty wall, I shook my head. I didn't know who the man in that picture was anymore and wondered if I ever really knew him. I walked back over to the closet and placed the picture behind the door.

I rubbed my forehead; I could feel my emotions trying to move front and center.

"No," I said, firm. "Not today."

I shook off the emotions and continued with my cleaning.

In less than an hour, the job was done. Standing in the middle of the floor, I surveyed my work. The room sparkled and even though it was he that walked away from our relationship, the room felt like he had never existed. It was *my* room now. It was bigger and emptier than before. I closed my eyes and plotted my next room.

"The garage, it's time to get it over with." I inhaled and exhaled deeply. Many times, I tried to get Jason to clean out the garage, but he never did. There was always some type of excuse as to why he didn't have time to clean it. Either he was too tired or he would get to it later. That was one more thing I had to add to the list that he didn't do. Whenever he did go down into the garage, he would just move things from one side to the other, or just do enough to make a pathway from the kitchen door that led to the back door.

I stood in the middle of the garage and shook my head. I didn't know where to start first. I was surrounded by Christmas boxes, big blue totes stacked on top of one another that were filled with kitchen appliances, old comforters, and boxes of clothes. Clapping my hands together as if I was preparing for a race, I pulled a hot pink bandana out of my pocket, wrapped it around my forehead, and tied it in the back. I went through the entire room to find anything that had to do with my marriage and put it all into a box and pushed it into a corner.

When we first moved in together, Jason didn't bring anything but his clothes and a few picture frames. He used to live with his mother, so he didn't have any furniture. Everything in the house belonged to me. Sure, he helped me put things together and fix things, but I paid for everything. The only things he had left in the house and the garage were a few pieces of clothing, coats and a baseball glove and bat that he bought himself for Christmas. I was tired and sweaty, but I was finally able to see the floor and park my car. I was proud of myself. The last thing that I needed to do was sweep the floor. Looking around the room, I round an old straw broom lying in the corner. I picked it up and frowned. I told Jason to throw this thing out months ago. As I started to sweep the dust and dirt from the floors outside to the driveway, the pieces of the broom started to break off. With every hit to the floor, one by one, the pieces popped off and flew into the air. I grumbled and swept the floor harder, causing more pieces to break. The harder I swept, the more pieces broke. I felt like I was sweeping him out of my life and into creation. I swept away the hurt and all the pain he caused me. I swept away the fake love I had for him and the constant feelings of being alone. All his lies were vanishing into the air. I was breathing hard, and my fingers ached from the grip I had on the wooden stick.

I took the broken and bruised broom and threw it in the garbage, closed the door, and walked back into the house.

"This is my house," I said as if I had built it from the ground up.

This was unreal. One week, I was married, and the next week I was single. It was surreal. I never thought this would be my life, but here it was and I was ready for my new beginning. The week was ending, and I finally had everything where I wanted it. Old pictures of Jason and I were replaced by pictures of me or my family. There were no traces of him and that felt good. I was ready to start my new life. Weeks passed, and I hadn't heard from Jason. I was angry that he had left me to handle everything on my own and not once did he call to offer to help me pay for any of the bills. My emotions were all over the place, and I didn't know how to handle them.

One day I was she-woman, and it was me against the world. I was strong and ready to take on any obstacle. The next moment, I was crying because I couldn't believe this was happening to me. I was behind on my bills and hated asking my parents for help. Hiding the secret of what happened between Jason and me became a full-time job. I was borderline depressed and had no one to talk to. I started to blame myself. How could I allow someone to come into my life who didn't care about me? Why did I continue to allow his financial issues to ruin my life? What else was he hiding from me? Was he doing drugs? Did he just use me for money? Did he use any of my family members for money? What was he hiding from me? I wanted to hurt him like he hurt me! I wanted these feelings to end, and I wanted to feel normal

again. I wanted to be loved the way my parents

loved each other. I wanted to believe that true love

was somewhere out there waiting for me. Trying to

embrace single life again was something new. In

the back of my mind, I knew there had to be

something in my life that had to change.

Something had to start looking up for me. I needed

peace.

But peace would come at a hefty price. All

I could think of was one thing. Something that I

never thought I'd ever do. The one thing my family

was always against. But it had to be done. I had to

get a divorce.

Five hundred dollars, six months, four days,

eleven hours, and fourteen emails later, I had

begun divorce proceedings. The process was

simple and easy. I didn't even have to talk to the

lawyer on the phone, and I didn't have to show up in court. We had no children and no real property together, so we didn't have to drag anything out.

Reestablishment became a number one priority in my life. I focused more on my work and started working extra hours to supplement my income. I hired a personal trainer, which also took my mind off of my past. I toned my abs and my legs while freeing my mind. I went back to school for my master's degree in childhood education. I kept myself busy and even enjoyed doing things alone like shopping or going to the movies, and most days, when either the sun was setting or it was waking up with the chirping birds, I'd find myself in a peaceful place. Nothing else mattered. Time was relative. And I was optimistic.

Chapter Eight

One year later, I sat on the bed studying for school. It was hard at first getting back into the rhythm of classes, but I took on the challenge with pleasure. I was happy to be on my own again, and even though paying bills was a challenge from time to time, I took it all in stride. After being served divorce papers, Jason went MIA. He never called, text, or stop by the house to see me. He had vanished into thin air. I tried calling his phone, but he wouldn't answer. I called his mother's phone, but she didn't answer either. Maybe he was out having fun spending his own money now that he didn't have any responsibilities. Maybe he was embarrassed and afraid of what I would say to him. Or maybe he found another woman to take advantage of. I soon realized I would never find out what Jason was doing with his money and why he couldn't pay our bills. I made peace with it, but hoped one day I would get a real answer. Wherever he was, I wished him well. I couldn't go on with my life unless I let it and him go. I didn't care anymore. It was meant to be. I was a single woman living my life again.

Just as I was about to shut off my computer, my cell phone started to ring. Jill Scott crooned about how golden her life was. Startled, I looked over and realized it was an alert for my Facebook account. Scrolling through the previous messages, I stumbled across a new message that shocked me. My lips parted and my eyes widened with curiosity. I hadn't seen this name in 25 years.

Looking back at the name a few more times, I read over the message.

Hi, it's Anthony. Your name has changed. What gives?

I sat up quickly and covered my mouth with my hand. My eyes traced over his name over and over. I couldn't believe what I was seeing. I hadn't talked to him since high school.

Only one year younger than I, Anthony played basketball and football at our high school, Madric Central. I used to watch him in his jersey as he walked past my locker on game days with the other football players. Because he was a star football player, everyone wanted to date him, including me. He walked around the school as if he owned it. He had the perfect set of teeth with a small gap in between and a smile that lit up the room. I was the shy skinny girl in high school, so I never let anyone know that I thought he was cute. I dared not tell anyone that I wanted to date a football player because I would be the laughingstock of the school. I never expected *him* to talk to me.

Standing six feet tall and full of charisma, Anthony's skin was a milk chocolate brown and his hazel eyes were dreamy. The fact that he was contacting me made me feel like a teenager all over again. My heart beat out of control as I tried to figure out whether I would respond or not.

"What the hell," I said, quickly typing a response.

I'm good! Hope you're well, too. Yes, my name has changed. I'm divorced now, how 'bout you?

Letting out a long hard breath, I sat the phone down and slowly rubbed the side of my face. I realized that was the first time I had spoken the word divorce to anyone. Before I could reach down to pick up the phone, he had responded.

"Wow, he's quick!" I said, smiling. I hadn't spoken or talked to any man since I had been married. It felt weird, sneaky and fun. I shrugged and waited to see what would happen next.

Do you mind if I call you sometime? He was direct with his questions.

Raising my eyebrows, I nervously touched each letter, one key at a time. *Yes, my number is 415-222-1125. Call anytime.*

Ten minutes later, lying down in the bed watching TV, I thought about what I did. I gave a man my number. I just spoke to another man. I just took my first step to being a single woman. Butterflies moved around in my stomach just as my phone started to ring. Startled, I looked over at the phone. My mouth fell open in awe. I couldn't

contain myself. It was him. He was calling me after

twenty-five years!

Ok, ok, get yourself together, I thought.
He's just a friend.

"Hey, friend," I said, trying not to laugh.

"Hey you, it's been a long time!" I could

hear the smile in his voice; his tone was low and

sexy, almost like Barry White. My heart was

beating way too fast, and I was blushing. It had

been so long that I had felt this way. And I was

giving myself permission to feel this way.

"Yes, so fill me in. Catch me up on all

that's going on, are you married," I said, waiting to

hear more of his sweet voice. I could remember

standing at my locker listening to him talk as he

walked by with his friends. His voice was still

dreamy. He sighed and began to tell the saddest

story I had ever heard. He said his wife cheated on him after six years of marriage. Seems that her emotional detachment from him couldn't be fixed because she was secretly seeing an ex-boyfriend behind his back for three years.

"Wow, and I thought my situation was bad," I said. With a soft tone, I gave him the short version of my situation. After a long sigh, I told him that although it was hard, I was happy to be on my own. And after living through years of lies, everything was brand new to me.

"You know, thinking back to high school, I remember always watching you walk down the hall with your books clenched to your chest," he said with a chuckle.

My mouth hung slightly open as shock took over me. "You watched me?" I had no idea that he was the least bit interested.

"Uh, yeah. You honestly thought I magically walked by your locker every day just because?"

I daydreamed and imagined his subtle gap in between his teeth as he spoke. "Well, that's funny. I never knew you even looked at me, or knew I existed, for that matter."

"Well, I'm glad that we're speaking. Are you dating anyone right now? Maybe we can finish our conversation over dinner."

I placed my hand over the phone and giggled like a teenager. This was amazing. Excitement took over my body as I danced around the room. Gaining my composure, I said, "Sure, I'd love to." I smiled ear to ear.

"Great, I'll text you with the details in a few. I'm excited!" He sounded giddy. We spoke for another hour before we ended the call.

One week and twenty conversations later, we were ready to go out on our date. The night he came to take me out to dinner, I was nervous. It took me an hour to find just the right outfit, which didn't give me much time to curl my hair or put on any makeup. Instead of arriving at our planned time of six in the evening, he came early at five.

When he rang the doorbell, I tiptoed to the door and peeped out the blinds to take a quick look at him. He looked even better now than he did in high school.

"Damn." I shook my head as I looked down and noticed his arms through his shirt. His muscles were bulging. I closed my eyes, exhaled and opened the door. And there he stood, a piece of heaven, flashing a Morris Chestnut smile. I grinned and reached out my arms to hug him. My face fell into the small of his arm and chest, and I inhaled his cologne. I didn't want to let go, but I did.

"Hey, I'm so glad to see you," I said as I pulled back and looked him over. He started to tell me about his drive over, but I didn't hear what he said. I saw his mouth moving, but all I could do was look at him very slowly from head to feet. I felt warm inside and turned on. I hadn't looked at another man in years, and I couldn't take my eyes off of him.

"Are you ok?" he asked, still smiling.

I blushed. "Oh, yeah," I said with a nervous laugh. "You ready to go?"

"Yep, let's do this!"

I grabbed my jacket off the bathroom door and walked back over to him. As I stopped to lock the door behind us, I smiled, took a deep breath,

and whispered to myself, "Thank you, Lord. This
is the first day of the rest of my life."

I couldn't get Anthony out of my head.
There was not a minute that we were not with each
other or talked to each other. We text each other all
day long and then talked on the phone for hours at
night after work. I told him my secrets, and he told
me his. I laughed and smiled. I was happy for a
change, and I didn't want the feelings to go away.
There were times when I felt this was too good to
be true. Maybe I was feeling this way because I
didn't get this attention from Jason. Or maybe it
was because I had left a miserable marriage of four
years. Whatever it was, I didn't want it to end, and
I was excited about the possibilities of dating
someone I had watched from afar twenty-five years
ago. I never thought I would ever feel this way as I

expected to be single for the rest of my life, but here was a new man who was giving me a feeling of happiness.

The more time I spent with Anthony the less I thought about what Jason put me through. We were inseparable. During the workweek, Anthony would come over at night after I got off work and stay over until it was time for me to go to bed. We talked for hours, laughed and watched TV. On the weekends, we went out for breakfast, lunch, and dinner. We never got tired of each other and started to miss each other when we were apart. I knew it was early in the relationship, but I knew our relationship was meant to be. Anthony constantly told me how much happier he was with me than anyone else he had ever been with. I didn't tell too many people that I dated Anthony because I didn't want to be judged about starting a relationship so soon after being divorced. I didn't want anyone telling me that I should wait before I dated again. I didn't want anyone acting like it was wrong for me to be happy again. To fall in such a trance with a man who wasn't Jason was new to me, but it was almost like I yearned for him to complete me.

Time flew and nine months of dating felt like three years of dating. I was beaming at my newfound relationship and realized I was falling for my new chocolate love drop. He was all that I had dreamed of, and my heart skipped a beat whenever I heard his voice. I've always wanted to gush over a man who made me happy. I've always wanted to tell the world how happy a man made me feel. When Anthony touched my face and kissed my lips, I melted. When we made love, it was so explosive that I couldn't get enough of him.

185

The way he held me, the way his body rubbed up against mine…I just couldn't control myself. I constantly wanted him.

My new relationship with Anthony brought me to a great revelation. There's an old saying that my grandmother used to say. People come into your life for a reason. I believe Jason was sent to me to allow me to realize what I was supposed to have in life. Peace. I realize I didn't have to settle for a certain type of man because there was no one else showing me attention. I realized that even though I was alone, life would still be ok. I didn't have to stay in a relationship trying to make it work because the world says it's the right thing to do. I was miserable for so long that it became my normal.

But now, being happy was my new normal. I was ready to finally experience the true meaning of love and all the possibilities that surround it. It was time to let the world know that I was with someone who really cared about me and was not going to tell me lies or hide things from me. It was finally my time to live.

Maybe I had to go through all of the bad luck and hard times just to get to the best time of my life with Anthony. I found everything I needed in him, and when I was with him, I saw a man who couldn't keep his eyes off of me. I saw a man who would go out of his way to make sure I had a smile on my face every time he saw me. Trust me, in the beginning of our relationship, I had a small wall up to protect myself. But somehow, somewhere along the way, he kicked the wall down, and my heart opened to love. I was filled with so much positive emotion that I didn't want to lose it.

When I looked at him, I couldn't help but smile. He meant so much to me. Tears ran down my face when I thought back to what I went through with Jason. I dried them as I realized that what I was going through now was true love.

Anthony and I were meant to be. I'd found my happily ever after and my soul mate. I'd found a man who loved me with every breath he took and caused me to lose my breath when I thought of him. He was protective, and most of all, he was my best friend.

He didn't lie from his heart.

He told the truth from his soul.

Here's a sneak preview of

Dangerous Indiscretions

"Shit!" The pain shot from my neck straight to my forehead. I thought I was about to pass out as my cellular phone vibrated and stopped me dead in my tracks. My ex husband's name Jason flashed across the screen as I tried to comprehend what was happening. "Why in the hell is he texting me?" I hadn't heard from him since I filed for divorce a year after he walked out on me. *"Hey there, just want to say I miss you. Hope I'm not bothering you."*

I took hard breath and let out a nervous laugh. Is he for real? I sat down at the kitchen table and stared at my phone. I didn't know what to do. My stomach was in knots. I had lost so much during my

189

marriage to Jason and after slowly getting back on my feet here he was popping up out of nowhere.

The pain moved from my forehead to my right temple and throbbed. I closed my eyes and tried to figure out my next move. Should I text him back? Did I even want to re-live what he did to me? Where is he? Does he have a job? My mind played Jeopardy and my phone vibrated again waiting for a response. I'll take what is deleting the message for $600, Alex.

Acknowledgments

When I began writing this book, I had no idea where it would take me. Thank the Lord I had people in my life to push me to do something that I never realized I had in me.

Makenzi, you were there from day one when I spoke my idea into existence. Thank you for being a great co-worker and literary friend. I have learned so much from you. Without you, this would not have been possible. Thanks for constantly listening to me and for giving me great advice. *High Five*

Danita, the day after my life turned upside down, you were one of the first people I called. You comforted me with your kind words and gave me one task: Write. And that is exactly what I did.

You didn't know that I kept that word in my mind, and I thank you for making that day a little better. *Air Hug*

Last, but certainly not least: *Anthony*, you came and turned my life around. I haven't stopped smiling since. *Thanks for saving my life!*

www.ingramcontent.com/pod-product-compliance
Lightning Source LLC
Chambersburg PA
CBHW031956040426
42448CB00006B/380